Preventive Photoshop

Take the Best Digital Photographs Now for Better Images Later

DOUGLAS FORD REA

Peachpit Press

Preventive Photoshop: Take the Best Digital Photographs Now for Better Images Later
Douglas Ford Rea

Peachpit Press
1249 Eighth Street
Berkeley, CA 94710
510/524-2178
800/283-9444
510/524-2221 (fax)

Find us on the Web at: www.peachpit.com
To report errors, please send a note to errata@peachpit.com

Peachpit Press is a division of Pearson Education

All photographs by Douglas Ford Rea unless otherwise indicated.

Development Editor: Amy Standen
Production Editor: Becky Winter
Indexer: Karin Arrigoni
Interior Design & Composition: Danielle Foster
Cover Design: Charlene Charles-Will
Cover Production: Andreas Schueller

Notice of Liability

The information in this book is distributed on an "As Is" basis without warranty. While every precaution has been taken in the preparation of the book, neither the author nor Peachpit shall have any liability to any person or entity with respect to any loss or damage caused or alleged to be caused directly or indirectly by the instructions contained in this book or by the computer software and hardware products described in it.

Trademarks

Adobe and Photoshop are registered trademarks of Adobe Systems Incorporated in the United States and/or other countries. All other trademarks are the property of their respective owners.

Many of the designations used by manufacturers and sellers to distinguish their products are claimed as trademarks. Where those designations appear in this book, and Peachpit was aware of a trademark claim, the designations appear as requested by the owner of the trademark. All other product names and services identified throughout this book are used in editorial fashion only and for the benefit of such companies with no intention of infringement of the trademark. No such use, or the use of any trade name, is intended to convey endorsement or other affiliation with this book.

ISBN 0-321-41096-3

9 8 7 6 5 4 3 2 1

Printed and bound in the United States of America

Dedication

I'm dedicating this book project to my parents; people built on the hard work ethic. I wish my Dad could read this today, but hope that he is doing so from above. And, to my Mother, I extend my heartfelt gratitude for her love and unwavering strength—both of which have been my inspiration.

Acknowledgements

I would like to give special thanks to several individuals for their help and suggestions over the years. There have been so many helpful people, I'm sure to overlook someone. First, I want to thank my colleagues at RIT's School of Photographic Arts and Sciences and School of Print Media who always stand ready to share ideas and suggestions. I will always remember and thank Professor Frank Romano for his advice, in particular, "the hardest part of writing your book will be the completing the table of contents." I thank my friend Bruce Fraser for his encouragement and sage advice by example over the past 15 years. Pam Pffifner, Senior Acquisitions Editor at Peachpit Press, who understands and appreciates the challenges educators face every day because she is one. It takes one to know one—thank you for your support and encouragement. My development editor Amy Standen, whose patience and encouragement went hand-in-hand with helping to coach this photographer's experiences and practices into words. I'd also want to thank Frank Butler at the MAC Group, Bill Pekala at NikonUSA, Dano Steinhart at Epson, Audrey Jonchneer at Kodak, Brian Ashe at GretagMacbeth, Dave DeMont at Applied-Image, Erik Sowder and John Baker at ExpoDisc, Michael Tapes at PictureFlow, John Wartman at Norman, Steve Upton at Chromix, Ken Boydston at Megavision, Doug Jensen at StormJacket, Lou Schmidt at Hoodman Corporation, and Trish Swords at Greg Gorman Photography. I would also like to recognize my three contributing student photographers: Jeremy Lips, Sarah Weeden, and Jessica Suworoff. Each did a great job.

Finally, I want to thank all my family, but especially my sons David and Andy. They are the blessings of my life. My sister, Donna Queen, who lives each day with more zest than the previous one. She's my hero. And for each and every friend who has supported me through the many facets of my career and personal life. To my late wife Annie and all that she brought to my life—it's immeasurable. And, lastly my wife Barbara for her loving and unwavering support through so many long evenings and short weekends. You always light up the room.

Contents

Foreword

I wish Doug had written this book ten years ago!

There are a great many Photoshop books on the market (for which I'm partly to blame), and one may reasonably ask if we really need another one. The short answer is, yes we do. The longer answer is that, despite its title, this is as much a book about photography—and in particular, digital photography—as it is a book about Photoshop.

Photoshop is an amazing tool, but when we spend too much time working in Photoshop, we run a real danger of getting carried away with our own cleverness. It's possible to fix a great many image flaws using Photoshop, and to display a great deal of cleverness in doing so. Unfortunately, our love of our own cleverness often makes us overlook the fact that if we'd spent just a little time thinking about what we were doing when we shot the image, our cleverness would be moot because we would have taken the image without the flaws we labor mightily in Photoshop to fix. Which when you think about it, is pretty stupid....

I first met Doug a little over 15 years ago at the Print '91 trade show in Chicago. Back then, the digital component of that show was one small hall, surrounded by other much larger halls full of behemoth presses, coating towers, bindery equipment, and other print manufacturing arcana too obscure to mention. On learning of my then nascent interest in digital photography, which in 1991 was very much in its infancy, Doug showed me a superbly subversive little magazine entitled "Esprit" which he explained stood for Electronic Still Photography at Rochester Institute of Technology, where he continues to teach and inspire new generations of photographers in his capacity as chair of the Photojournalism department.

The work featured in the magazine was fascinating, and demonstrated that despite the limitations of the then current technology, digital photography could offer a vibrant new look at the world we live in. But even then, it was obvious that the seductive option of "fixing it in Photoshop" occasionally led his students to overlook photographic fundamentals. Doug's teaching position has made him uniquely qualified to point out the pitfalls of relying too heavily on Photoshop. It's great to experiment when you're a full-time student, but not so great when you have to deliver on a deadline.

In *Preventive Photoshop*, Doug covers the fundamentals, but more importantly, he helps you develop the indispensable habit of pre-visualizing the result before you press the shutter, and instills a thorough understanding of the things that are best done in the camera, the things that are best done in Photoshop, and the difference between the two. Armed with this knowledge, you'll spend less time trying to fix things in Photoshop that should have been handled in the camera, so you'll get better images with less work.

If you want to spend more time shooting and less time wrestling with pixels, you need this book.

Bruce Fraser
San Francisco, 2006

What Is Preventive Photoshop?

1

HOW MANY TIMES have you heard the phrase "I'll just fix it in Photoshop," and then discovered that "fixing" an image means hours in front of your computer? While Adobe Photoshop is a marvelous and powerful tool, the facility with which it lets us alter images has resulted in sloppy photographic habits—poor lighting, bad exposure, deathly shadows, and overblown highlights. Wouldn't it be better— and easier—to take the time to shoot the photograph right in the first place, thus minimizing the backbreaking hours hunched over a keyboard? Wouldn't you rather capture your image correctly so you can use Photoshop for fine adjustments and (dare I say) have a lot more fun?

I'm a huge fan of Photoshop. I use it on each and every picture I've photographed with my digital camera. But I've also learned to be smart about what role Photoshop plays in my workflow, and to do as much as possible in the camera to avoid wasting time in Photoshop. Photoshop, for me, is a means to an end. I take what is my best possible image with my camera, and then move it to Photoshop to optimize it for print and/or Web presentation.

Thinking it through from the start can save you a lot of time and effort in photography. What to do and when to do it are the big questions you'll face as you get started. The rule, most of the time, is that you should do most of what you can in-camera rather than fixing it in the darkroom—or electronic darkroom, as the case may be.

Of course, there are some things better done in the computer, after a photograph has been made. Most photographers, for instance, sharpen their images in Photoshop, rather than use in-camera auto sharpening modes. After all, how you will print your image (i.e., the size, printer type, material, etc.) will define the best way to sharpen it (**Figure 1.1**). Let's look at some of the main topics we'll be discussing in this book, and whether those tasks are better done in-camera or in Photoshop.

(Credit: Jeremy Lips, Jessica Suworoff, Sarah Weeden, and Lynn Wilson)

Figure 1.1 Getting the image you want requires understanding what should be done in-camera, what can be polished in Photoshop, and when the two work hand-in-hand. This photo shows how Photoshop can contribute to the photographic process during a live shoot.

Lighting

Photography is all about light. Whether we find it, make it, or modify it, successful photography all comes down to light (**Figure 1.2**). The quality of light in a given scene determines the choices a photographer must make to best convey his photographic message. We often need to modify lighting to get the point across in our pictures. If we didn't, the shadows might lack sufficient detail, creating impenetrable black areas, or the highlights might appear blown out, resulting in unnatural white spots. So we adjust lighting when we must.

Figure 1.2 *"In the right light, at the right time, everything is extraordinary." (New York City–based artist Aaron Rose)*

You can adjust levels and curves in Photoshop to your heart's delight, but it's challenging to turn a badly lit photograph into a good one in Photoshop. Furthermore, each lighting adjustment you make in Photoshop creates a change in the tonal relationships within that photograph, which means that you'll spend a lot of time compensating for problems these adjustments create. The impact of these changes is not always bad, but it can make your photograph a less accurate representation of the scene as you saw it.

You can see this discrepancy best in the shadows of a photograph. Unless you account for lighting problems at the time of capture, the shadow regions of your image will lack detail. Photoshop can do a lot of things, but it can't create the detail that your camera missed in the first place.

The bottom line: Get your lighting right before opening Photoshop.

Tones and Toning

Photoshop is better as a polishing tool than a problem-fixing tool, so it's always best to start with as few problems as possible. Examples of this kind of polishing are Photoshop's levels, curves, and other toning tools found under Image > Adjustment (**Figure 1.3**). Toning is a way of describing how bright areas of an image are. In the digital arena, this corresponds to levels of gray. Even when an image is viewed in color, the underlying digital foundation is still gray, or shades of it.

Figure 1.3 Photoshop's levels and curves tools are great for fixing tone problems.

Thanks to Photoshop, minor toning problems—an overexposed shadow, for example—have become quite addressable in the digital darkroom. Even if your image doesn't have obvious tone problems, Photoshop's tools may make the difference between a good photograph and a better one.

In some ways, Photoshop's toning tools mimic the "Zone System" invented by Ansel Adams for his black-and-white film-based photography. First, Adams would define his photographic scene in terms of *zones* (or tones), ranging from a solid black (0) through a range of grays, to a solid white (9). Having analyzed the tone values in this way, Adams would then expose and develop his film in combinations that maintained the proper balance of all the shadows, midtones, and highlights. Ultimately, he produced a negative that, when printed in the darkroom, replicated the scene just as he had envisioned it (**Figure 1.4**). It was a beautiful photographic process. If Adams were alive today, however, I believe he would be thrilled with all the digital photographic and post-photographic tools at his disposal.

Figure 1.4c gives you an idea of how Adams may have previsualized a landscape, breaking it down into zones. As he captured the image, Adams would try to maintain detail in the shadows. Later in the darkroom he would develop the film to keep details in the highlights.

Today's digital photographer has the same goals but takes different steps to achieve them. We most often expose to maintain detail in the highlights and then process our images in Photoshop to restore the shadows. Digital photography puts the Zone System—or something very much like it—

Figure 1.4a Witnessing a beautiful landscape, like this one can be a very moving experience. How our mind and eyes respond to this scene, though, is very different than what happens in a camera.

Figure 1.4b I've added a grayscale bar or ramp at the bottom of this image to show the range of tones in this photograph.

Figure 1.4c Here's the image again, with each tone identified.

at your disposal. Making good decisions in the field or studio will save you time in the darkroom—just as it did in Adams' day—whether it's an analog darkroom or a digital one.

The bottom line: Capture highlights and shadows correctly, and then polish them in Photoshop.

Special Effects

Special effects come in three forms: those conceived before the photograph is made, those done afterward in the computer, and those that require a combination of the two. The special effects strategy you should use depends on what is easiest, what will provide you with the most control, and what will, ultimately, yield the best results.

As with lighting, it's often best to attempt to achieve special effects in front of the camera's lens. However, Photoshop has a toolbox of filters that can add a sense of movement to an image as well as a host of other special effects.

Regardless of the opportunities or challenges at hand, keep your mind open to working in either or both photographic and post-photographic environments.

The bottom line: Consider the type of special effect you want, and experiment—first with your camera's settings and then in Photoshop.

Sharpening

Sharpening an image correctly is like getting your shirt pressed before you wear it. It delivers crisp, clean lines that are pleasing to the eye. Still, too little or too much sharpening makes for unsatisfactory results. Sharpening works by enhancing the contrast in specific regions of a photograph where there is a change in brightness levels. Just as you wouldn't want to over- or under-do the contrast in your images, the same applies to sharpening.

When you shoot in JPEG mode, your camera sharpens your image automatically, every time. All cameras made with solid-state imaging devices (known as CCD or CMOS sensors) that are inherently unsharp. Digital cameras rely on sharpening because they must blur the image slightly to be able to correctly interpret color during processing. Many of today's cameras give you a chance to adjust the sharpening algorithms. My advice is, if you can turn your camera's automatic sharpening off, do so. It's much better to do most, if not all, of your sharpening in Photoshop (**Figure 1.5**). In Photoshop, *you* decide how much sharpening you want, and where.

The bottom line: Sharpen your images in Photoshop.

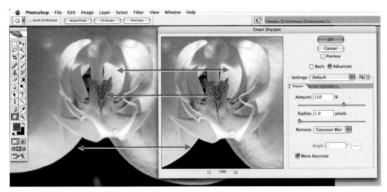

Figure 1.5 *This image was made with the sharpening turned off. The image on the right shows how the scene's detail can be finessed with Photoshop's Smart Sharpen filter.*

Summary

Photoshop is not always the best solution for addressing photographic challenges. What we do behind the camera is just as, if not more, important as anything we do afterward. What's most essential is that you think it through before you start a photographic session. Consider what you can do before or during your session to make the best photograph. Then decide which problems you'll be able to address later in Photoshop and which you won't. You'll make much better photographs, save time and frustration, and spend your Photoshop time more effectively and efficiently.

Understanding Digital Capture

2

BEFORE YOU CAN LEARN how to minimize your reliance on Photoshop, you need to be able to take better pictures. Taking better photographs means understanding how digital cameras work and how to use their settings. While digital cameras have a lot of smarts built in, you won't get the best results letting the camera make all your decisions for you. You need to make the right choices at the right time.

If you feel confident in your camera skills, feel free to skip this chapter. However, it's always good to have a refresher course.

Photographers who come from a traditional film background are familiar with terms like exposure and metering—concepts that may be new to some digital photographers. Film shooters, on the other hand, never really had to worry about sensor size and image resolution.

Today's photographer navigates between film tradition and digital innovation. To make sure we are all on the same page, let's review common camera controls and the role they play in capturing the best possible digital images.

DEPTH OF FIELD

Depth of field is also a function of focal length. A longer focal length will yield less depth of field. Keep in mind that on a small digital camera—one with a tiny sensor—your lens probably has a very short focal length, so getting shallow depth of field is difficult with a small-sensor camera.

ISO is a leftover from the days of film, and is a measure of how sensitive a piece of film is to light. ISO in a digital camera works the same way. A higher ISO number means your camera is more sensitive, and therefore doesn't require as much exposure to yield an image. With a higher ISO, you can shoot in lower lighting conditions while still using a shutter speed that's fast enough for hand-holding. Take note that as you increase ISO your images will get noisier.

Exposure: Shutter, Aperture, ISO

There are three different mechanisms for controlling exposure: Shutter Speed, Aperture, and ISO.

Shutter Speed controls the amount of time that the shutter is held open. Faster shutter speeds mean less light strikes the sensor and slower shutter speeds allow more light to pass through. Some smaller cameras lack a physical shutter, and simply turn the sensor on and off for the specified amount of time. Shutter speed also gives you "motion control." By choosing a slower or faster shutter speed, you can blur or freeze motion respectively. Be warned, though, if you choose too slow a shutter speed, it will be difficult to hold your camera steady, and your resulting image will be soft, or outright blurry.

Aperture controls the size of the iris that's built-in to your camera's lens. A smaller iris stops more light, while a larger aperture allows more. A smaller aperture also yields an image with deeper depth of field (more of the image in focus) while a larger aperture yields shallower depth of field (see "Depth of Field" sidebar). Apertures are measured in f-stops. The larger the number, the more light that you're stopping. So, f/16 is a smaller Aperture than f/8. If you want less depth of field, then you'll select an aperture with a lower number (because a wider aperture yields less depth of field).

A camera's ISO number is the measure of its sensitivity to light. When you increase the ISO settings on your camera—for example, moving up from 50 to 100, 200, or 400—you're amplifying its signal, like turning the volume up on your radio. Higher ISOs allow you to make photographs in low-light conditions, for example. But here's the catch: if you turn up the volume too high on that radio, you're going to hear static. Likewise, the higher you tune your camera's ISO, the greater level of noise you'll see in the captured image. That increase in noise is based on your particular camera technology, sensor, built-in camera noise reduction firmware, and several other under-the-hood factors. But there are a few simple things you can do to reduce image noise:

- Use the lowest possible ISO your photographic situation will permit.

- Avoid long exposure times if possible. Many solid-state sensors react less favorably with long exposures and, consequently, generate higher-than-normal amounts of image noise.

- If your camera has an image-sharpening option, make test photographs at different ISOs set to both the on and off positions. If the sharpening increases the amount of noise, keep this option in the off position. (You can always do a better job of sharpening in Photoshop anyway.)

Photoshop does have some good noise reduction filters, so if you choose the wrong ISO, you might be able to save the image. But simply doing it right the first time will save you a lot of time. If you're working with just one image, reducing noise in Photoshop might not be such a big deal. But if you need to produce six or seven, you're facing at least another hour of work in front of the computer—versus an adjustment you could have made on your camera in seconds. Also, keep in mind that color tends to degrade at higher ISOs, so that's one more tricky adjustment you'll need to make later in Photoshop.

Let's look at a couple of ways you can test what your camera is capable of doing to reduce noise.

Testing your camera's noise-reduction feature

1. Mount your camera on a tripod or the sturdiest stand you can find.

2. Make a series of photographs at the full range of ISOs available in your camera—for example, ISO 100, 200, 400, 800, 1250, 1,600, and higher.

TIP

Planning on buying a new digital camera? When buying a new camera, test its noise levels at different ISOs. Then, select a camera system that gives you acceptable results within the ISO range you must work within. Bring along a memory card to your local camera store. Make photographs of the same subject using each available ISO on a particular camera. Bring the memory card back to your computer and take a closer look.

3. Make two exposures at every ISO, one with the in-camera High ISO noise reduction in the off position and one in the on position.

4. Move the images to Photoshop and inspect them at 100 percent magnification. Compare the two images of each ISO side by side. How are their noise level, sharpness, and color quality? Do the camera settings help or hurt your image quality? (**Figure 2.1**)

Figure 2.1 The image on the left, shot at ISO 100, has less noise than the one on the right, shot at 1600.

Testing your camera's long-exposure noise-reduction feature

1. Mount your camera on a tripod or your sturdiest alternative.

2. Make two exposures at each shutter time of $1/8$ of a second, $1/4$ of a second, $1/2$ of a second, one second, two seconds, all the way up to a minute if possible—one with the in-camera long-exposure noise-reduction in the off position, one with it in the on position.

3. Move the images to Photoshop and inspect them at 100 percent magnification. Compare the two images of each shutter speed side by side. How are their noise level, sharpness, and color quality? Do the camera settings help or hurt your image quality?

Reciprocity

All three of these parameters—Shutter Speed, Aperture, and ISO—have a reciprocal effect on each other. For example, if you choose a faster shutter speed, there will be less light striking your camera sensor, and your image might end up underexposed. To compensate for the faster shutter speed, you'll want to switch to a wider aperture, or a faster ISO.

Similarly, if you decide you want a blurry background in your image and open up your camera's aperture, then you'll run the risk of overexposing your image. To compensate, you'll need to choose a faster shutter speed.

Exposure modes

Your camera probably provides several different methods for controlling exposure. These exposure modes are usually selected with a dial on the camera or from a setting inside the camera's menu system. Different exposure modes will give you different levels of control. Most cameras will have some variation of the following:

- Fully Automatic: In this mode, your camera will decide *everything*. This includes shutter speed, aperture, ISO, even white balance and when to use the flash. For the most "idiot-proof" shooting this is the way to go.

- Program Mode: Program mode selects aperture and shutter speed automatically, but lets you choose ISO and white balance. In addition, program mode may let you apply Exposure Compensation (we'll learn more about this later). This is the best mode for general shooting.

- Aperture Priority: Lets you select the aperture you want. The camera will then select a corresponding shutter speed that will yield a good exposure. Priority modes also give you full control of ISO and white balance.

- Shutter Priority: Just the opposite of Aperture priority. Select a shutter speed, and the camera will select a corresponding Aperture.

- Manual: Gives you control of *everything*. Shutter speed, aperture, ISO, and white balance. Manual mode gives you the ultimate control, but also lets you get your images wildly wrong if you're not careful.

SCENE MODES

In addition to the normal shooting modes, many cameras have additional "scene modes" that bias the cameras' exposure decisions to yield better results in particular situations. For example, your camera might have a Landscape mode that automatically chooses smaller apertures for deeper depth of field, ensuring good focus. Other scene modes might include:

- Sand and Snow, which will automatically overexpose to properly render bright tones such as fields of sand or snow.

- Portrait mode, which will choose a wider aperture to create a soft background.

- Sports mode, which will automatically choose a faster shutter speed to freeze action.

In most scene modes you'll have no control over ISO and possibly limited white balance control. In addition, you may not be able to use the flash at all.

EXPOSURE COMPENSATION

Most digital cameras have an exposure compensation control, which lets you dial in up to two stops of over- or under-exposure, usually in $1/3$-stop increments. The great thing about exposure compensation is it allows you to make relative exposure adjustments without having to concern yourself with reciprocity issues or worrying about specific aperture or shutter speed settings.

So, for example, if you decide that you need to brighten a scene, you can simply dial in a positive exposure compensation.

Metering and Exposure

As you've already seen, exposure—that combination of shutter speed, aperture, and ISO settings—determines not only how bright or dark your overall image is, but also lets you make artistic decisions about how much of your image will be in focus, and how rapidly moving elements in your scene will be frozen.

Your exposure decisions begin with your camera's meter. When you press the shutter button on your camera halfway down, your camera's built-in light meter analyzes your scene and calculates an appropriate shutter speed and aperture. Your camera probably provides a choice of several different metering modes:

- Matrix metering (sometimes called "evaluative metering") takes readings from across your entire scene and averages them together to come up with a valid exposure.

- Center weight (sometimes called "partial metering") does the same thing as Matrix metering, but when averaging it adds more weight to the center part of your image. Since your subject is usually in the middle of the frame, this often yields a better exposure. Center weight metering is particularly useful for backlit situations, where you want to ensure that the subject in your foreground is not plunged into shadow.

- Spot metering meters off of a very small part of your image— often a circle that's only 5 to 10 degrees. Spot metering is particularly useful for scenes with a very high dynamic range, where you want to ensure that you don't overexpose one particularly bright section.

Knowing how to select the right meter settings is an essential part of getting good exposure. Spend some time with your camera's manual and learn what your metering options are and how to select them. On a smaller point-and-shoot camera, you might have fewer options.

Light and Tone Reproduction

Making JPEG photographs with a digital camera is a lot like making photographs with transparency or slide film: you really have

Figure 2.2 Normal exposure is an averaging of brightness information.

Figure 2.3 Two stops overexposure gives you detail in the shadows at the expense of information in the highlights.

Figure 2.4 Two stops underexposure gives you detail in the highlights at the expense of losing information in the shadows.

to nail the right exposure the first time because you're only capturing so much information. Raw images, as we'll discuss shortly, allow more flexibility. If you're working in raw, your image probably will be usable as long as you get within the four-stop range of an accurate exposure—between two stops overexposure to two stops underexposure (**Figures 2.2** through **2.4**).

For years, I've been repeating this mantra to my students who make either JPEG or TIFF photographs: expose for the highlights and image process for the shadows. Expose your image so that you can see the highlights clearly; if your shadows lack detail, you can adjust them later in Photoshop. The nature of digital photography means that overexposing detail in an image often means losing it forever. Highlight areas hold important detail, and they are where the observer's eye usually goes first.

Think of a coal miner covered with coal dust coming out of a mine. Your eye goes to the highlights for all the important information, but most of the scene is in the shadows. In low-key scenes like this one, it's especially critical that you expose for the shadows, making sure to preserve as much detail in the most important parts of the image. To every rule, of course, there are exceptions. One such exception is an extremely bright scene. If you want to photograph a skier on a bright sunny afternoon against a backdrop of freshly fallen snow, the opposite rule applies. A scene like this is all highlights, and it's the highlights where the viewer will find the critical detail. Therefore, in a case like this, you must expose for the highlights and process for the shadows.

TIP

Extraneous light hitting the front surface of the lens can be a real problem, especially for digital photographers. The culprit is the glass plate guarding the camera's solid-state sensors. This plate is more reflective than film, and therefore more likely to produce lens flare and aberrations. The best way around this is to use a professional lens compendium such and a Lindahl Professional Lens Shade, ideally with a vignette mask installed. This is a good idea for both studio and location photographers.

Both of these scenes have a high dynamic range—both scenes contain many thousands of gray levels, a dynamic range beyond any digital camera's capability. The closest thing to it, however, is raw capture. The more information you take at the time of capture, the more detail you'll be able to pull out later in Photoshop.

Another solution to difficult lighting situations is to modify the lighting ratio. This is nearly impossible on location outdoors or in any other naturally lit environment. But in the studio, photographers routinely modify their lighting ratio by adding or subtracting light. They add light by using additional lighting or reflectors and subtract lighting by using "gobos," or go-betweens, which are translucent or opaque objects. Light sources that that are hard or specular in nature, like bright sunshine or a car's headlight, give higher contrast and, as you might expect, yield less shadow and highlight detail. Softer, diffuse lighting, like light through a lampshade, gives lower contrast, creating an image with more shadow and highlight detail.

The following examples illustrate that in the studio it's best to light your subject correctly to avoid long hours of working in Photoshop. **Figures 2.5a** through **2.8b** detail a set of low-key and high-key images of the same subject. If you light things correctly in the studio, you can save a lot of time attempting to achieve the same results in Photoshop.

Figure 2.5a *This high-key photograph was lit correctly in the studio, with a variety of lights and gobos (which subtract light) so very few Photoshop adjustments were necessary. Time spent in Photoshop: approximately 30 minutes. (Credit: Jeremy Lips)*

Figure 2.5b *This image dramatizes where both additive and subtractive creative lighting was applied in the studio to achieve Figure 5.7a.*

Figure 2.6a *The highlights and shadows in this high-key photograph were created in Photoshop. Time spent at the computer: over three hours.*

Figure 2.6b *This image dramatizes where Photoshop was used to create shadows, highlights, and background gradient. The numbers indicate the areas that needed toning.*

Figure 2.7a *This image was lit in the studio to build the tonal ranges that you see in this low-key photograph. Very few Photoshop adjustments were necessary.*

Figure 2.7b *This high-contrast illustration dramatizes how both additive and subtractive studio lighting creating shadows, highlights, and the background gradient. Time spent in Photoshop: less than 30 minutes.*

Figure 2.8a *The highlights and shadows in this low-key photograph were created in Photoshop. Time spent in front of the computer: over four hours.*

Figure 2.8b *This high-contrast illustration dramatizes where Photoshop was used for both additive and subtractive studio lighting in an attempt to create shadows, highlights, and background gradient. The numbers indicate the areas that needed toning.*

Internal Image Settings

Your camera has many internal settings that control how it processes images when you're shooting in JPEG mode. These settings let you control everything from how image-processing characteristics such as contrast, tone, saturation and more, to how much sharpening is applied to the image. Some cameras provide a very simple interface that allows you to select a setting for each parameter. More advanced cameras provide more advanced interfaces for customizing your camera's built-in processing. For example, some let you define custom "tone curves" that control brightness and contrast in your image.

Be warned, though, that this internal processing "uses up" some of the editability of your images. If your camera does a big contrast change on your image, you're going to have a hard time removing it later, if you want. However, if your goal is to get finished images out of your camera, these options can be very handy—provided you understand ahead of time what they're going to do.

Consider the following scenario: you're going to go shoot a friend's wedding, and the bride has asked if there's any way they can take the digital pictures with them on their honeymoon. Since weddings usually yield hundreds of images, spending a lot of time editing the images is not practical, and what's more, you'll only have a few hours to turn around the entire batch.

The wedding is going to be held in a park at four o'clock in the afternoon, so a few days before the wedding you take a friend to the park and do some test shooting. You shoot a number of shots with different combinations of settings, and then go back home. A reception is planned for the evening, and that will be indoors, so you do some test shooting with your camera's built-in flash.

By analyzing the results, you decide that setting the contrast to +1, the saturation to 0, the Brightness to +2 and leaving the sharpening where it is, you consistently get excellent results that look good in print when shooting in daylight. Next you analyze your flash pictures and determine that setting contrast to -1, saturation to +1, brightness to 0 and leaving the sharpening alone yields great

IN-CAMERA IMAGE SETTINGS AND RAW

The wedding-shoot scenario described will work on any camera that's set to shoot JPEG images. If you're shooting raw files, things work a little differently. Since your images are not processed inside the camera (this is one of the points of raw shooting—no in-camera processing—so you get the "purest" data possible for your own editing efforts) any image processing settings that you make are irrelevant. Usually.

Some cameras, such as the Nikon D80 store in-camera image-processing settings inside the metadata of raw files. If you process the raw image using Nikon's Capture NX, then your files will have your proscribed edits automatically applied, meaning all you have to do after a shoot is convert your raws to JPEGs—no additional editing required to get the results you want!

results for indoor flash pictures. Your camera allows you to define different sets of parameters, so you store each of these configurations in a separate set.

On the day of the wedding, you select your outdoor set for shooting at the wedding, and then quickly and easily switch to your indoor set when the wedding party moves indoors.

When the shoot is over, you copy your images to your computer, and quickly browse through them to find and select your best images. You burn these to a CD, hand them off to the bride, and you're done! Because your camera has taken care of all of the processing, and because you took care to crop properly in-frame, you don't need to do any additional processing.

Raw vs. JPEG Images

Raw and JPEG are worlds apart. A raw image contains all the information a camera can capture "uncooked" by the adjustments your camera makes automatically. JPEG images, on the other hand, contain only a fraction of that information. There are advantages to each. Because raw images are true digital negatives, they make for much larger files. JPEGs, on the other hand, are relatively small and quick-recording. But if you've got the space and memory available, shoot raw. Raw gives you far more options later, when you take the images back to your computer. Some cameras permit you to shoot and record in both raw and JPEG simultaneously (**Figures 2.9** and **2.10**). This can be very useful since it gives you both a camera's true digital negative as well as fast-to-access JPEG files for quick edits, transmission, or use on a Web page. But beware: the dual recording option will take up more space on your camera's memory card.

Another drawback to raw files is that they can be a bit more complicated to upload onto your computer. This is because, unlike TIFF or JPEG, there is no standard raw format—one camera's raw image may not be the same as another camera's raw image. If you're using Photoshop, you're taken care of: Photoshop includes

---

THE RAW TRUTH

- Raw images are true digital negatives. They hold more information about the photographic scene than some of us will ever use, but it's nice to know that it's there if you need it.

- Raw images are generally two or more stops forgiving in terms of over- and underexposure.

- Raw images let us revisit and adjust the image's white balance, color temperature, color space, tint, gamma, contrast, saturation, noise, and much more when we're in Photoshop.

- Raw files are much larger and cumbersome than JPEG files, and sometimes require extra software.

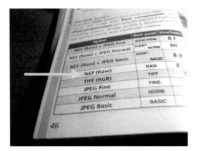

Figure 2.9 *Your camera manual will tell you exactly what kind of files your camera can capture. It's easier and faster to get this information from your manual than your camera. Go here first.*

Figure 2.10 *Finding the same information on your camera's LCD screen may require going through a lot of menus.*

a raw converter called Camera Raw (this is described at length in Chapter 6, "Processing Raw Images") that can open most cameras' raw files. If not, you'll need a stand-alone raw converter to move your images to your computer. Your digital camera probably came with its own raw converter and both Mac and Windows come with their own built-in raw converters so you'll be able to open (but not edit) your raw files. Because Photoshop can't communicate with your camera directly, you'll use your camera's raw software to convert the images as they come out of your camera and onto your computer. Once they've been converted, you're free to transfer them into Photoshop.

Camera Color Mode Settings

Most digital cameras don't have very sophisticated color mode setting options, but several camera systems allow you to choose between sRGB and AdobeRGB, two color spaces that you can choose for your camera to work within. The choice you make will make a big difference later, when you begin your work in Photoshop. Given this choice, it's best to select AdobeRGB, which offers a much broader color gamut than sRGB (**Figure 2.11**). It's much better to bring *more* information with you into Photoshop than *less*.

Some digital cameras let the user compensate for tone and color balance automatically in JPEG images (remember that in raw images, you are in control of image quality). In other words, a photographer can—based on what she sees on the LCD screen— set her camera to make automatic tone and color adjustments (**Figure 2.12**). This isn't always a good thing to do.

Adjusting your camera's tone and color settings to accommodate specific areas within the image may cause problems elsewhere in the image. It's much better to shoot at as close to neutral as possible and save the adjustments for later, when you have the time and freedom to experiment. There's almost nothing you would do with your camera's color settings that you can't do better in a raw converter or Photoshop.

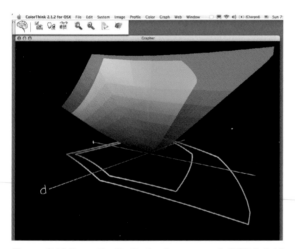

Figure 2.11 Here, the limited color space of sRGB is laid over the much broader color space of AdobeRGB.

Figure 2.12 Many of today's digital cameras allow you to choose a color mode in the setup menu.

Selecting a Resolution

While your camera may bill itself as a "5-megapixel" or "8-mega-pixel" camera, it probably offers several resolution settings that are *lower* that that maximum resolution. For most situations, you'll want to shoot at your camera's maximum resolution, simply because more pixels affords you more image cropping and output possibilities. So, even though you know that you're only going to put your images on the Web, if you're shooting a once-in-a-lifetime event, you should probably set your camera on its highest resolution, because you may decide one day that you'd like to print those images.

Also, higher resolution provides you with the option of cropping a small part of your image and enlarging it to a desirable print size.

However, if you're in a hurry to get your images posted to the Web, and you don't want to bother with re-sizing them in your computer, you can lower your camera's resolution, so that it saves out at a much smaller size. Depending on your camera's output choices, this smaller size may be exactly what you need for uploading.

Some cameras allow you to select resolution and compression as separate options. As you probably already know, more compression means a smaller file, but lower quality—you'll see lots of ugly, blocky patterns in your image. If space is not a concern, then leave your compression setting set to best quality, while you change the resolution to the size that you want for your final output.

Note that your camera may not offer an output size that is exactly what you want for your Web postings. In this case, you might as well shoot at full resolution, since you're going to have to resize your images anyway.

Initial Camera Settings

When you go into any shooting situation, you'll want to give some thought to your initial camera settings. Some of these settings are things that you'll set once and leave alone for the whole shoot (resolution, JPEG or raw, color mode).

White balance will be changed every time you change a lighting situation. If you're shooting JPEG and using in-camera image settings, and providing you established different parameter sets for corresponding situations, then you'll want to make certain that you've selected the right set of parameters for that situation.

When it comes to the actual moment of shooting, you'll alter your camera's setting based on the needs of the shot. If you have specific exposure needs—shutter speed control, for example—then you'll want to choose a shooting mode that affords you the control you need to make the exposure adjustment that you want. From shot to shot, you might also change metering modes to make certain that your camera calculates the proper exposure.

For all of this to work smoothly, you need to know where your camera's controls are and how to operate them, so that you can quickly get your camera configured for the situation. A mis-set control—which can lead to bad exposure, blurry images, wrong depth-of-field, or bad color—causes problems that have to be corrected later in your image editor.

Summary

Understanding what your camera's controls can yield in terms of final image quality can help you make intelligent decisions while shooting, so that you get images that look the way you want without additional help. Then, when you need to open Photoshop, you'll have the best material available to work with.

Seeing Your Pictures in Advance

3

THE OLD SAYING "what you see is what you get" (WYSIWYG) comes to mind every time I click the camera's shutter in front of a scene like the one in **Figure 3.1**. If only it were true. When it comes to digital photography, the more likely experience is, "what you see is *more or less* what you get" (WYSIMOLWYG). That's oftentimes my reality.

If I want to capture what I see, or as close to that as possible, I must make some good decisions prior to shooting. I'll base these decisions on what I see, how I see it, how I want to interpret it and, ultimately, how I want others to see it.

Figure 3.1 *All too often, what you get is not what you see. Look at the camera's LCD. This is a good example of WYSIMOLWYG, or "what you see is more or less what you get."*

Unlike the landscape painter who very carefully considers the scene behind his canvas and then expresses those impressions with his brush, the photographer is forced to make critical decisions in an instant. He must understand the light; he must focus selectively, frame effectively, and accurately expose the image. All of these decisions must be made in a short period of time, and there's usually only one chance to make them right. The photographer may not get a second chance, because conditions may have changed from one moment to the next.

I, like most photographers, want you to read my photographs in the way I intended. I want to influence your interpretation. I may want you to reach many of the same conclusions I did—to enjoy the scene I've photographed, to learn from it, be moved by the moment—or perhaps I have another goal in mind. I also want you to be able to interpret the image and take from it what you want. To accomplish any of these goals, the right choices must be made.

Photographing What We See

Photoshop offers incredible tools for correcting and adjusting exposure, tone, and color. And it provides the ability to create retouchings, composites, and selective edits that would be impossible using film and a darkroom. However, very often an image is unusable not because of problems with its exposure or color, but because it's poorly composed. In fact, a well-composed image that has exposure or color problems is often much more interesting and usable than a perfectly executed shot of a boring composition.

With a Crop tool, like the one found in Photoshop, you can often correct or "re-compose" your images after-the-fact. By changing the crop of a picture, you can focus the viewer's eye, and change the balance of the elements within your frame. Of course, cropping requires a trip into your image editor, something we're trying to minimize.

By learning a few shooting habits, and paying more attention when shooting, you can get your compositions right in the camera, and avoid a trip to your image editor.

In this chapter, we'll be looking at a few things you need to keep in mind to get the best shot that you can straight out of your camera.

Composition

Every picture has its own compositional needs, so it's difficult to lay down hard-and-fast "rules" of composition, but there are some guidelines you can follow.

- Guide the viewer's eye. A good composition is one that helps the viewer's eye find its way. Lots of things will attract the viewer's attention, from changes in contrast or color to the arrangement of foreground and background elements. When composing, your goal is to manage these elements so as to lead the viewer through your picture to your subject.

- Build from left to right. Westerners tend to "read" a photo from left to right, just as they read text from left to right. So, if all of the interesting parts of your image are on the left-hand side, the viewer may not pay much attention to the rest of the scene.

- Create balance. If you have a close up of a lion's head in the lower-right corner of your image, then you'll usually need to balance this strong element with something in the opposite corner. You don't have to create balance with a similar element. Open space, a strong color, a bright highlight—all of these elements can serve to balance each other.

- Think in thirds. Imagine your image divided into a grid that is three rows high and three columns tall. If you place the elements of your image at the intersection of these grid lines, you'll usually get a fairly well composed shot.

- Watch for juxtapositions. We've all suffered from this mistake. You shoot a beautiful portrait outdoors, and only when you get home do you realize that your subject has a telephone pole sticking out of their head. Remember: images are flat! You need to pay attention to how the 3D world you're living in will be squished into a flat image.

WHAT TO LOOK FOR WHEN YOU PREVIEW YOUR IMAGES

- How's my composition? Are there aspects of my framing that I need to change?

- Is my color working? Do I have to make adjustments with the white balance setting on my camera?

- Is my subject in focus?

- Do I have sufficient depth-of-field?

- Is my image exposed correctly? Are the highlights, midtones, and shadows in balance?

- Are my highlights blown out?

- When capturing moving subjects: Am I stopping the action correctly?

CHECK YOUR EDGES

One of the easiest ways to improve your compositions is to pay attention to the edges of your frame. Line up your shot the way you want it, then take a moment to trace your eyes around the edge of the frame. Paying attention to your image's edges will help you spot bad juxtapositions, and will help you see your image more objectively, making it simpler to spot compositional troubles.

Choosing an exposure

Once you've framed your shot, you're ready to meter. Press your shutter button down halfway to tell your camera to meter your scene. If your composition is dependent on depth of field control—maybe you want to blur out the background to bring focus to your subject—then you'll need to modify your camera's meter reading to opt for a larger aperture.

As discussed in Chapter 2, you might need to change your camera's shooting mode to a priority or manual mode, or use a special portrait mode to achieve the depth of field effects that you want.

ADJUST YOUR EXPOSURE

If your scene contains things that are really dark, then you will need to use your camera's Exposure Compensation control to underexpose your image slightly, to render the dark things with their true tone. Similarly, if you're shooting things that are really white, then you'll need to overexpose.

Exposure Compensation allows you to easily dial in these over-exposures and underexposures, even if you're using another control to manage your depth of field concerns.

If you apply proper compensation to your exposure, then the light and dark tones in your image will be accurately exposed, saving you the trouble of making tonal adjustments later in Photoshop.

Use your camera's histogram and metadata

Fortunately, with a digital camera you don't have to do as much guesswork as you had to do with film. Thanks to your camera's LCD screen you can easily check your composition as soon as you shoot, while your camera's built-in histogram display and meta-data screens allow you to make an informed assessment of your exposure decisions. To go even further, try a tethered system that connects a camera to a computer monitor. In addition to giving you more information about your images, these tools—used effec-tively—can save hours of work in Photoshop later on.

The liquid crystal display (LCD) is not a WYSIWYG device. It is a WYSIMOLWYG device, and a rather small one at that (**Figure 3.2**). Still, we could hardly get by without them. Thanks to LCDs, photography is now practically real time: We can preview our photo-graphs almost instantly on the back of our digital cameras. For better or worse, LCD screens allow the photographer to begin the process of editing almost immediately after the photograph is taken (Figure 3.2). We have the ability to do timely, effective, almost real-time editing as well.

Figure 3.2 The LCD gives you a very small preview of what you'll see on the computer display and the final print.

Figure 3.3 Once you push this button, it will be next to impossible to recover the images you've just eliminated.

However, many photographers make snap judgments based on what they see on the back of their digital camera, and often those decisions are wrong. The image is so very small on an LCD, and viewing conditions may be challenging. Coupled with the fact that most cameras boost the contrast and saturation of their LCD images to make them visible in bright light, judgments may be skewed. Sometimes a photographer moves too quickly to delete images, based on what he perceives to be a mistake and attempts to recover that data may prove difficult or impossible.

The LCD is a useful tool to check that your image is in focus. This takes time, however, and is usually not advisable after the shooting session begins. But the time you spend looking at your LCD is time spent away from making photographs. If you're looking at the back of your camera, you're not following the action in front of the camera (**Figure 3.3**). Performing such tasks as zooming in and out on a captured image can interrupt the rhythm of seeing and capturing images in an effective way. The playback zoom—the one on your LCD used for reviewing images—is much better used for test images, taken before the shoot even begins, so that you'll be confident that your images are focused well (**Figures 3.4** and **3.5**). Or use the playback zoom after your photo session has ended to confirm that you got the results you wanted.

LCDs can also be helpful for bracketing your exposures. By bracketing, I mean doing a small series of normal, over-, and underexposures of your subject. For instance, if your meter indicates that you have a basic exposure setting of f/8 at $1/250$ second, you might bracket this first exposure with a second one at f/8 at $1/125$ second, and then a third at f/8 at $1/500$ second, and then quickly compare the results on your LCD. This will give you a much better chance of getting the best exposure for a particular photographic setting.

Figure 3.4 Most digital cameras allow you to magnify an image with the simple click of a button.

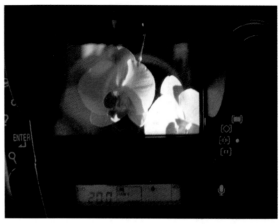

Figure 3.5 Magnifying an image allows you to make sure your image is in focus.

Many cameras include an auto-bracketing feature that will sequentially bracket exposures for you at predetermined settings. These settings can also be useful in still-life photographic sessions, when you have as many chances as you need to review your bracketed images and adjust accordingly. If you are photographing people or moving objects, then you'll have to perform your bracketing test before your photographic session begins.

How do bracketing and magnification relate to Photoshop? Well, think of them as anti-Photoshop devices. The better you use zoom tools (despite all their faults, they're still better than nothing) and bracketing tests, the less time you'll spend making sweeping and technically difficult changes in Photoshop later.

USING YOUR CAMERA'S HISTOGRAMS

Histograms and highlight warnings are built into many of today's digital cameras, which show up on your LCD screen at the click of a button. A histogram shows the relative distribution of pixels of the various brightness levels in an image ranging from shadow areas on the left to highlight areas on the right. An image with no shadows will show a histogram with minimal data on the left; a histogram with no highlights will have a graph with minimal data on the right (**Figures 3.6–3.8**).

WHAT IS AN F/NUMBER?

An f/number (also referred to as an f/stop) is the ratio of the lens focal length to the diameter of the lens opening. For example, a 100mm lens divided by a 50mm opening would give an f/number of 2, or 100mm/50mm = f/2. The larger the f/number, the greater the depth-of-field. Depth-of-field is the distance both behind the subject and in front of the subject that appears to be in focus. This is important because a photographer must be confident that the important subjects within the scene are in focus.

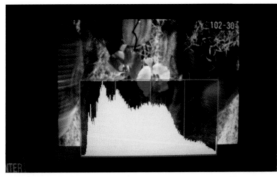

Figure 3.6 Histograms describe an image's range of shadows, midtones, and highlights. Looking at the histogram (yellow area), this image appears to be well exposed, with a broad tonal range.

Figure 3.7 A histogram with most of the information appearing on the right side of the yellow graph indicates an image with overexposure—one that lacks shadow detail.

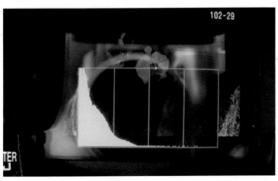

Figure 3.8 A histogram with a spikew, or cliff, of information on the left side of the graph indicates underexposure. This image probably lacks sufficient highlight detail.

Histograms give you the information you need to take a better image next time around. Let's walk through a typical histogram experiment.

1. Set your camera's f/number and shutter time for a normal exposure.

2. Make an exposure. (Remember: It's only a test shot!)

3. Press the camera's image playback button. Your image appears.

4. Press the camera's multiselector, speed dial, or info button to reveal the image's histogram.

5. Set your camera's f/number and shutter time so that it will capture a greater-than-normal exposure.

6. Make a second exposure.

7. Press the camera's image playback button.

8. Press the camera's multiselector or speed dial to reveal the image's histogram for a second time.

9. Set your camera's f/number and shutter time to capture a less-than-normal exposure.

10. Make a third exposure.

11. Press the camera's image playback button.

12. Press the camera's multiselector (or speed dial) to activate the camera's histogram for a second time.

13. Compare the different images and decide what the best exposure settings are.

USING YOUR CAMERA'S HIGHLIGHT WARNINGS

Highlight warnings pick up where histograms leave off by warning us if we're in danger of overexposing a scene's highlights. They reveal overexposure, allowing you to take care of the problem before it occurs.

The real issue is how accurate your histograms and highlight warnings are. Many photographers today rely almost exclusively on in-camera histograms and highlight warnings to ensure that their exposure values (most specifically the highlights) are in check (**Figure 3.9**). This is one area where Photoshop's tools are superior. They don't replace the histograms you would access in Photoshop. An in-camera histogram, for example, might not catch the exposure problems seen in Figure 3.9. Still, in a pinch, LCD-based histograms and highlight warnings are an effective means of finding out whether exposure changes must be made on future shots.

Figure 3.9 The highlighted (in this case, black area) of this image lacks sufficient detail. These areas might be very difficult to identify on an LCD, or by looking at the image's histogram on the camera.

Reading Metadata on Your Camera LCD

Camera metadata is available from your digital camera's LCD almost the moment you capture an image, and, although it's limited, this information can be a great resource for understanding and improving your photographs (**Figure 3.10**). The metadata you see on your camera's LCD screen describes your images' ISO settings, white balance, aperture, and more.

Still, maneuvering through screens of metadata on your camera LCD can be difficult. It usually involves a series of micro switches and other navigational keys, many of which are small and hard to handle. Having cold hands or big thumbs and fingers can make finding metadata a challenging task indeed.

Figure 3.10 A variety of camera metadata is available on your LCD screen, including date, ISO, color space, white balance, and more. (Photo credit: Jeremy Lips)

The first place to look as you begin learning about metadata is your camera's manual. Pick an image from among those on your memory card and follow the steps in the manual to find out more about it. Notice how your camera records ISO settings, white balance, metering, exposure information, tone, and more for each and every image it takes.

Using Metadata

Perhaps the best time to look at your metadata is right after you take an image, to confirm that you chose the settings you intended. I can think of plenty of situations where accessing my metadata would have saved me time and energy—even saved me the trouble of having to repeat an entire shoot. Had I accessed metadata on my camera's LCD screen before returning to my digital darkroom, I might have avoided the following scenarios:

- My depth-of-field—the sharpness from the nearest to the farthest object in the photographic scene—is insufficient. Did I use an aperture that was too large?

- The image's focus/light/color looked fine on my LCD, but proved a disappointment later, when I finally saw it in my raw converter or Photoshop.

- I thought I was using the correct white balance, but my JPEG pictures seem to have an overall color balance that's not what I intended.

- I thought I had selected a fast shutter speed to freeze the motion as I photographed moving subjects. But now that I see the image on my computer's screen, it looks blurry.

- I thought I'd set my camera to the AdobeRGB color space, but once I was back at the computer, I discovered it was still in sRGB mode.

All of these problems could have been easily prevented in my camera's setup menu. Instead, I lost hours of irreplaceable photographing time, and doomed myself to many long sessions in front of Photoshop.

In addition to serving as a diagnostic tool, metadata can also give you a good idea of how to fix a problem. If your metadata tells you that you chose the wrong ISO, for example, it's likely your image will benefit from noise reduction or color correction in Photoshop. If metadata reveals that your white balance was not what it should have been, you'll want to use your Photoshop or Camera Raw white balance tools. If you see a problem in your image, metadata can often tell you what went wrong and, therefore, what to adjust for when you're in front of the computer.

Getting Simultaneous Feedback with a PC

Histograms on an LCD are great, but they can't compare with the experience of seeing your image on a full-sized monitor. Your computer monitor may be anywhere from 12 to 30 times the size of your camera's LCD (**Figure 3.11**), and it can give you vastly more information about detail, white balance, color, noise level, and many other important things, all of which will affect how you take your next image. I often connect my camera to my computer monitor, in what's called a "tethered PC system," to give me instantaneous, detailed feedback on my images.

Figure 3.11 The size of your LCD screen makes it hard to spot detail on an image, even with the use of magnification. Compare this to the rich, detailed image a computer display can provide.

Figure 3.12 A tethered system gives the photographer immediate access to all kinds of useful information about the image he's just captured.

Figure 3.13 A tethered system provides the fastest feedback possible on an image, as well as access to many tools for making objective image evaluations.

Getting large-scale feedback from a photographic session can be valuable in many instances. It brings the photographer full circle in the picture-making process, by showing results quickly and in a more compelling format. A tethered system allows a photographer to assess the image's technical information and metadata—the hidden identifying information attached to each image—its composition, lighting, focus, and depth-of-field (**Figure 3.12**). The computer monitor becomes the second viewfinder in the photographic process, an expanded view of what's been done right and what's been done wrong (**Figure 3.13**).

Wiring a camera to a PC depends on the input and output (I/O) that your equipment provides, but today's modern computers have USB 2.0 ports and some have FireWire. Both formats have the necessary bandwidth to move images pretty effortlessly. Once connected, you'll start to see your digital camera as an additional hard drive on your computer's desktop.

In some cases you can simply drag and drop images from your camera to a designated folder on your computer; in other cases the images are moved from camera to computer with the click of a button. The tethered system frees you from having to remove memory cards or use a card reader to move images.

Setting up a Camera-Computer Connection

If you're working in a studio a tethered system is the best way to get accustomed to working your computer and your camera at the same time (**Figures 3.14** and **3.15**). Remember that it's also possible—and something I recommend—to take your tethered PC out into the field as well. It's a bit trickier to haul all that gear to a location shoot, but it can be more than worth it. Out in the field, a wireless connection is one way to go, but in most cases a wired system should work just fine, especially as wireless systems are more complicated to set up and can suffer the inconsistent connections similar to that feeling that plagues any cellphone user from time to time. In either case you will need a camera with tethering ability, which describes of today's Digital SLR cameras. Here's a quick primer on how to set up a tethered system.

Figure 3.14 Your digital camera is basically just another computer peripheral. A wired or wireless system, such as the one shown, will help you get better results.

Figure 3.15 A tethered system can look as simple as this.

CONTROLLING YOUR CAMERA WITH YOUR COMPUTER

Some cameras come with software that allows you to control the camera via the computer, in addition to the camera controls. With a Nikon D-SLR, for instance, you would use Nikon Capture Software, while a Canon D-SLR requires the Canon Software. Both software packages provide powerful image capture and editing capabilities—you can even set exposure time and f/number settings via your computer. Both packages allow you to import images directly into the computer and make tone, color, and cropping adjustments. This software also makes it easy to move images to Photoshop.

1. Place your computer and digital camera on a safe and secure base.

2. Select the appropriate cable, making sure it's long enough to connect your computer to your camera without limiting your motion more than you're willing to put up with.

3. If you haven't done so already, install your camera software on your computer.

4. Connect either the USB or FireWire cable between your digital camera and computer.

5. Install a light-blocking hood on your computer monitor for better previews.

6. Set your exposure time and f/number, either on your camera or through your computer if your software allows it (see "Controlling Your Camera with Your Computer").

7. Make a test exposure.

8. Review the image on your camera's LCD. Look at image focus and exposure quality. Use your histograms to see if the exposure is well balanced.

9. Now review your image on your computer using your digital camera's software. Check sharpness and exposure again, as well as image noise and detail within the shadows and highlights. Use your software's information dialog box to see if the numbers support your visual impression of your image. Export the image into Photoshop to get even more information.

SENDING IMAGES TO A PORTABLE STORAGE DEVICE

Let's say it's not possible to connect to a PC where you're located, or perhaps you simply don't need to. You're left to save your images on your camera's memory card. Once that's full, you can't make any more photographs. There's another option: the portable storage device (**Figure 3.16**). (I refer to them here as PSDs, not to be confused with the Photoshop format .psd.) Strictly speaking, this isn't a tethered system. You won't be able to see the images on the PSD instantaneously as you take them, and you won't have access to Photoshop, either. Still, PSDs are a handy option, and they give you much more information than your digital camera can. PSDs are small and, in some instances, inexpensive, but most models let you review images and associated image data (i.e., exposure information), and some even allow you to inspect image histograms. Furthermore, they provide a secure backup for your images.

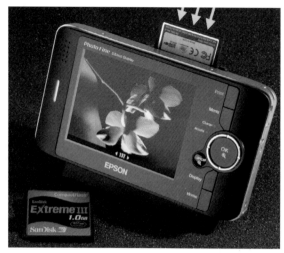

Figure 3.16 Personal storage devices are an easy, inexpensive way to enhance your view of the images you've just made. They also back up your images to an album on the portable storage device (PSD) hard drive. Later, you'll move the images from the PSD to your computer's hard drive shown here is the Epson PhotoFine.

Challenges and Solutions of Connected Systems

Connected systems are a great way to get detailed and timely feedback on your images, but they do complicate your photography workspace and introduce a new set of challenges.

- Challenge: Seeing the laptop screen is a problem in bright lighting conditions.

  I've found myself and other photographers with jackets or blankets draped over our computers, looking much like Ansel Adams or any other early-20th-century photographer trying to see his camera's ground glass. Add the difficulty of handling a mouse—or worse, a touchpad—and the situation can start to feel downright hopeless. For those of you wearing glasses, it's even worse.

Figure 3.17 A light-blocking hood, such as a Hoodman, will help you see your display clearly in bright conditions.

Figure 3.18 One versatile solution is a camera/computer bag such as the Tenba Gemini, which also functions as a display hood.

The answer is to make or purchase a monitor hood that can block extraneous ambient lighting without interfering with your keyboard (**Figures 3.17** and **3.18**). In a pinch, you can even make one yourself, using foam core, cut and trimmed to fit your display (**Figure 3.19**). Attach the hood to your display with two-sided tape or a Velcro-type material.

- Challenge: The camera needs to be placed in a position in which a photographer can't stay—for example, it may need to be high in a rafter, in a dangerous area, or in a location that the photographer must leave to attend to other things.

Connect your camera to your PC and operate the camera remotely. A camera's capture software will allow you to work at a distance, and you'll reap all the other rewards of a tethered system as well.

- Challenge: Rain or hot coffee gets on your keyboard.

We can control a lot of things in photography; weather is not one of them. There are some protections for cameras (**Figure 3.20**), but laptops are another story.

If you shoot out in the elements, find a laptop that is element proof. Considering how often photographers injure their laptops in the line of duty, having a laptop that can weather a flash rainstorm is more than a blessing.

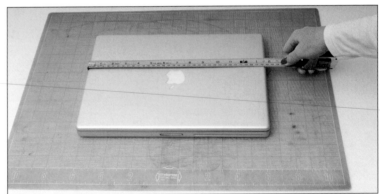

Figure 3.19 You can also make your own inexpensive screen hood from foam core. First, measure the screen dimensions. Next, cut some foam core to size. Now score and bend the foam, and finally, apply it to the screen with two-sided tape. This is a short-term solution—a homemade screen hood won't last as long as commercial products.

If you already have a laptop, there are a few ways to weather-proof your computer. I've used large disposable, resealable plastic bags effectively, although typing on a plastic bag-encased computer is not always an ergonomically pleasant experience.

- Challenge: Computers, cords, PSDs, camera equipment—what's the best way to set all this stuff up?

Find something that is light, portable, sturdy, and reliable to use as a workbench, although make sure it can withstand windy conditions and the occasional bumping. If your car is nearby, sometimes the trunk makes an excellent workspace (**Figure 3.21**).

- Challenge: There are no outlets in the middle of the wilderness.

Photographers have moved from depending on film to depending on batteries or AC outlets. Have you ever counted the number of rechargeable devices you use? Used to be that only our flash units asked for a recharge. Now it's cameras, flashes,

Figure 3.20 A Vortex Media's Storm Jacket, or something like it, will protect your lens and camera in inclement weather conditions.

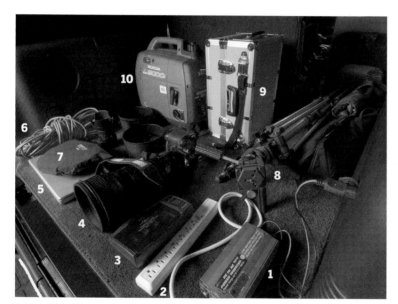

Figure 3.21 The trunk of your car is a great place to work at your computer, refresh your battery gear, and transmit images to your client or home office. I use a combination of AC/DC inverters and, for long sessions, a portable generator. The generator keeps me from running my vehicle's battery down. 1) DC/AC inverter, 2) power strip, 3) battery charger, 4) camera gear, 5) laptop, 6) extension cord, 7) Hoodman E2000 laptop sun shade, 8) tripods and stands, 9) camera and lens cases, and 10) portable generator.

computers, portable studio strobes, cell phones, image storage devices, PDAs, Family Radio Service radios, DC/AC converters...and the list continues to grow every year. I often carry one kit that includes nothing more than just extra batteries and chargers. Sometimes I feel like we spend more time charging batteries than making photographs.

Figure 3.22 While shooting on location, I use whatever electricity I can find in the area, or produce my own with a portable generator.

Figure 3.23 Now that cameras and lenses are used in concert with computers and a lot of electronic accessories, organization is all the more important. Here, a photo backpack bag and a Tenba Gemini camera/computer bag keep things in place.

Out in the field, power is always a problem, especially on long shoots when you drain all your batteries. Here are your power options, such as they are:

- Locate a 110-volt power source and establish a safe, AC connection.

- Convert 12-volt power to 110-volt power using a DC/AC inverter. Most cars have one or more 12-volt power outlets, or you can draw power directly from the battery using alligator clips.

- Make power with a fuel-powered inverter or a generator (**Figure 3.22**). Solar options are also available, which are useful for backcountry trips.

- Buy more batteries.

I use a generator to handle the power needs of my devices and an inverter for battery recharging in my vehicle.

- Challenge: Your bag is bulging with gear.

Photographers often have a plethora of bags in their midst, but what works best will vary from one photographer to another (**Figure 3.23**). I use a combination of solutions: traditional camera bags, backpacks, camera/computer combo bags, and traditional computer bags.

Unless I'm only carrying a single camera and computer (which is almost never the case), I often like to use a combo camera and computer backpack.

KEEPING ALL THOSE WIRES UNDER CONTROL

- Zip ties: These disposable restraints make it easy to hold your wiring in place. They come in various lengths, so you can pick the length you need. Simply wrap your wire to a support, zip it, snip off the excess length, and you're done.

- Wire snips: A pair of small wire snips is great to have around for cutting wiring restraints when you must change things around. Wire snips are also safer than utility knifes, which too often cut things you don't want cut.

- Cable ties—invaluable! These small, reusable restraints keep your wires neat and tidy. They are meant as temporary restraints, though. You'll use them, reuse them, perhaps lose them, and then buy some more.

- Duct tape and gaffer's tape: The old standby is more useful than ever. Although not exactly attractive, tape is particularly useful for covering wires in high-traffic areas of the studio. At best, it's a fast and temporary way to keep wiring out of harm's way.

- Floor cord covers, on the other hand, are the ideal way to keep from tripping on loose cables and cords running across a walkway or behind a computer cart. They cover, hide, and protect cords and cables while keeping floors clear and safe for equipment and foot traffic.

See **Figure 3.24**.

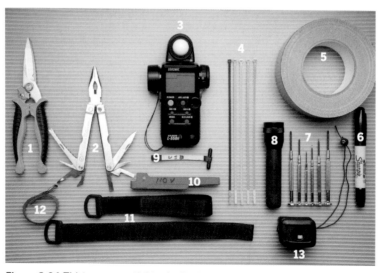

Figure 3.24 *Thirteen essential tools: 1) wire snips, 2) multitool, 3) light meter, 4) multipurpose ties, 5) duct tape and/or gaffers tape, 6) permanent marker, 7) jeweler's screwdrivers, 8) small flashlight, 9) elastic ties, 10) medium Velcro wraps, 11) large Velcro wraps, 12) small Velcro wraps, and 13) Hoodman SLR Pro cap.*

- Challenge: I've got digital cameras with wires leading to computers and computers with wires leading to displays, hard drives, printers, networks, UPSs, and power sources… Space is getting tight!

  Every studio is different, but organization is key, especially when you're working with a tethered system. **Figure 3.25** shows one approach to creating a safe and efficient work environment.

In my opinion, every photographer should consider using a connected PC, no matter where he works. In the studio, Photoshop is the photographer's primary postphotographic production tool; you can count on using connected computers there. But Photoshop can be just as useful in places we never thought to take a computer.

The more you use a connected PC on location, the more adept you'll become at using it in a nondisruptive way. Yes, it takes some practice. There will be awkward moments, maybe even some near catastrophes, but in the end, a tethered system will help you make much better pictures. Find a PC that works for you on location. Load it up with your digital camera's software and Photoshop. Now you're ready to embrace photography in a more meaningful way than ever before.

Figure 3.25 In this well-organized studio workspace, a rubber wire channel near the photographer's feet protects both him and his flash sync cable.

Summary

In digital photography, often "thinking it through" includes not only good planning, but also using the right tools to see whether you're taking the images you want. Visual displays, camera LCD screens, and computer monitors—and Photoshop are connected at the hip; the better you understand the photographs as you're taking them, the less work you'll have to do in Photoshop later on. Look, read, experiment, and design for yourself the best possible workflow.

Casting the Right Light

4

CAMERAS CAN DO AMAZING THINGS: tell a story, make an advertisement or fine art, record memories of family and friends, even help attain scientific advances. But all of these achievements depend on one element more than any other: light. Photoshop can do a great deal to massage the kind of light we failed to get at the time of capture, but nothing replaces the real thing.

As you photograph, you'll be thinking about tone, color, and lighting types. If at all possible, it's always best to get the right light at the time of capture, and by applying a few ground rules to those three elements, you'll produce better photographs. But despite your best efforts, you may end up with lighting mistakes. The underlying goal here is to do as much as possible at the time of capture to avoid having to fix things later in Photoshop.

Figure 4.1 Foveal vision gives only the narrowest view of our subject. Peripheral vision is the soft area around the foveal vision.

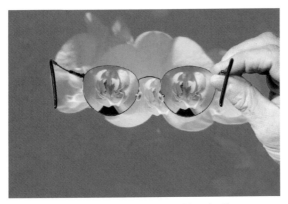

Figure 4.2 Stereoscopic vision provides depth.

Figure 4.3 A camera can't discriminate like the human eye (Figure 5.1); the entire field of view is sharp.

Human Vision vs. Camera Vision

Human vision is a mixture of many physiological and psychological factors that, together, allow us to see a scene subjectively, reacting differently to the elements within it that are meaningful to us. Our complex visual system (**Figure 4.1**)—combines foveal vision—the narrow, detailed area right in front of us—and peripheral vision, the areas to the left and the right of our foveal vision, where we detect shape and color but not detail. Meanwhile, our two eyes provide us with a stereoscopic view of our subjects (**Figure 4.2**), giving us depth perception. As all this is taking place, a complex system of rods and cones makes fine, instant adjustments to how we perceive light around us.

Our eyes and brain work tirelessly at defining as much detail, tone, and color as humanly possible, coupling what we see with what our mind understands about the environment before us (**Figure 4.3**). This is why I believe that there's a photographer in every one of us. Our eyes detect subjects and light in combinations that have an immediate, emotional effect on us. We are moved by what we see, even without a camera. All of this is possible because of light and how we perceive it.

Capturing this experience through a digital camera requires an understanding of how cameras work. The solid-state sensors that digital cameras employ in place of film are more sensitive to the red end of the spectrum than the blue end. In fact, these sensors are so sensitive to light that they pick up light we can't even see, such as infrared light, and depend on filters to limit their sensitivity. Bad lighting leads to more Photoshop work than just about anything else. Most tonal corrections—localized brightening, global brightening or darkening—could be prevented if you simply took care with your lighting.

Generally speaking, location photography is best served by available lighting. That, after all, is how we see things, and we want our images to turn out the way we see them. Unfortunately our camera sees things in a more objective way than we do. Our eye has the ability to scan a scene—to see tones and colors in a subjective fashion. Our mind also discriminates between what's important and unimportant in a scene. We value or devalue what we see within the camera's viewfinder.

No camera holds a candle to the eye's iris, which automatically and instantly opens and closes like a camera's aperture to see detail with clarity under different levels of light. Our eyes do this constantly in high-contrast environments, but a camera has no such intelligence; it can't discriminate. Cameras average the scene's tonal and color information based on their metering systems, or according to the manual settings we select for them. That's fine when it works, but it can play havoc with our minds when it doesn't. If an image looks different from what you saw through your viewfinder, it's probably because you expected your camera to act like your eye and capture all we see.

Supplemental lighting can make the information in the scene more readable by the viewer. For instance, an on-camera or off-camera electronic fill flash, useful for photographing high-contrast scenes, also allows us to see shadow details more clearly. Other times, we might subtract light from the highlights using some type of opaque object—what's referred to as a *gobo*, or "go-between."

Lighting, good or bad, can be either a friend or foe, but it's not something you want to leave in the hands of Photoshop. If at all possible, a photographer should address lighting deficiencies at the moment of capture, rather than attempt to fix things later.

Digital cameras prefer full-spectrum daylight color temperature light sources; in other words, they're calibrated to work best outdoors on a sunny day. For that reason, it's a good idea to use artificial light sources that most closely resemble daylight, such as electronic flash, high-frequency fluorescents, or HMI (hydrargyrum medium-arc-length plus iodide) lighting systems. If at all possible, avoid tungsten lighting sources.

Figure 4.4 Photographer Sarah Weeden took on a daunting 10-f/stop range in brightness and color temperatures ranging from 2,600k to over 7,900k. She captured a single exposure and then color balanced it using using Photoshop adjustment layers. (Credit: Jeremy Lips)

Working with Mixed Lighting

Mixed lighting usually means a combination of two or more sources of light with differing color temperatures. It can be a big obstacle for any photographer, and a near-constant one for those who work outside of a studio. If mixed lighting is something you deal with often, a color-temperature meter may be a necessity. Color-temperature meters are expensive, but they allow you to quickly and objectively determine the quality of light you're in, whether it's cool, warm, or something in the middle.

Once you've identified the color temperature differences, you should first set your camera's white balance for the dominant lighting source. Next, there are a few routes to take (**Figure 4.4**). One is to map out the various lighting sources within the scene and make multiple exposures of the scene, to be merged together in Photoshop later (**Figures 4.5a–4.5e**). **Figure 4.5f** is the result of this image merging. The second strategy is to adjust off-colored regions of the image in Photoshop. This method entails using color-correction techniques, selections, paint-brush work, and adjustment layers to color balance the scene. **Figure 4.5g** is the results of color-correcting a single exposure in Photoshop.

Figure 4.5a Here, a color meter was used to read the daylight temperature areas. Sarah set an exposure that allowed her to capture the highlight details. (Credit: Sarah Weeden)

Figure 4.5b With the help of a light meter to read the skylight area, an exposure was found to capture the highlight detail.

Figure 4.5c After a color meter read the temperature of the skylight region, the camera was set with a white balance of 7,900k.

Figure 4.5d After a color meter rated the temperature of the fluorescent lighting, the camera was set with a white balance of 3,600k.

Figure 4.5e After a color meter read the temperature of the incandescent lights at the bottom of the frame, the camera was set with a white balance of 2,600k.

Figure 4.5f Result 1: This image is a composite of the different color temperatures captured.

Figure 4.5g Result 2: Here, Photoshop was used to bring out blue/purple hues at 5 percent, and to adjust the saturated yellows.

Using an Electronic Flash

Harold E. Edgerton, who invented the electronic flash in 1931, would be proud of the impact that his invention has had on contemporary photography. Just about every digital camera comes equipped with a built-in flash. Professionals frequently use both specialized on-camera and stand-alone strobe systems in their everyday work. The quality of an electronic flash is also better suited to the particular mechanics of a digital camera, but we can't see the exposure quality of our electronic flash until after the picture is captured and displayed. One can zoom in on the camera's LCD screen for a closer look, but that's only a rough estimate.

Just about every high-contrast photographic situation will benefit from a fill flash, or fill light. Fill lights give you extra detail in the shadowy areas, but they can also be helpful for the rest of the image, too. Experiment with your flash (either on camera or external) with the power level set to ¼, ⅛, and ¹⁄₁₆. After some testing, select a power setting that complements your ambient light exposure. The flash may be all you need to brighten your shadows and add a small catch light to the highlights. This is most critical in JPEGs, as a balanced tone scale is not something you'll be able to easily re-create later in Photoshop.

Flash can be essential to getting a good exposure. However, just as you can overexpose or underexpose your image by choosing the wrong shutter speed or aperture, you can overexpose or underexpose your image by misusing your flash.

Here are some tips for getting better results from your flash:

- Know the range of your flash. Your camera's manual will include a range specification for your camera's built-in flash. Look up this number and remember it. Then pay attention to it when using your flash, especially if you're using a small camera. The flash units on small cameras have a very limited range—sometimes as short as 10 feet—and anything outside of that range will not receive any illumination from the flash.

- Learn about the different modes on your flash. Your camera's built-in flash probably provides several different modes such as auto, fill, and red-eye reduction. Consult your manual to learn how to select these modes, and how they perform.

- Find out if your camera has Flash Exposure Compensation. Most digital SLRs (and some point-and-shoot models) include a Flash Exposure Compensation feature that lets you brighten or darken the flash by dialing in an adjustment in ⅓-stop increments. So, if you shoot a flash exposure, and your camera's histogram indicates that your highlights are overexposed, you'll use Flash Exposure Compensation to lower the flash output to bring the highlights back under control.

- Use it or lose it! Flash is not just for indoors. If you're outside and someone has an annoying shadow on their face because they're wearing a hat, or standing under a tree, turn on your flash.

TIP

When shooting, a simple white piece of cardboard or foamcore might be all you need to prevent a trip to Photoshop. A white reflector will often allow you to reflect enough light onto your subject that you don't need to use a flash. Or, if you are shooting with a flash, a reflector can help you even out the flash exposure on your subject.

Summary

Lighting is the most important component of photography, and also one of the most difficult. Test your digital camera under different lighting situations—electronic flash, bright sun, continuous studio lighting—and keep notes on your results. And if you haven't already, consider adopting a tethered system to help you make the most of your photographic moment.

Creating Effects
In-Camera

5

WHILE I ENJOY the creativity and flexibility
Photoshop brings to my photography, I find that
too often we rely on the software to achieve what we should
have done in the camera. I wonder if we've forgotten what is
possible with a variety of camera techniques that perhaps some
of us, raised in a Photoshop world, never learned.

An important part of "Preventive Photoshop" is remembering
what's best done in the camera and what's best done in
Photoshop. Given all of Photoshop's filters and toning tools,
it's tempting to apply special effects post-shoot in front of the
computer. Instead, consider these creative effects that you can
do in-camera.

When you're wondering how you might spend less time in Photoshop, bear in mind that a good number of features are there to help you correct problems that started in-camera. In other words, simply looking at Photoshop's feature set can often help you figure out what you need to do in-camera so you don't spend time working in Photoshop.

In this chapter, we're going to look at a number of Photoshop features that you can easily avoid by simply learning to create the same effects in-camera, rather than in Photoshop.

Softening Images

Photoshop contains a number of very sophisticated blur controls. Using the Blur filters (located under Filters > Blur) you can create simple or complex blurs that make your image appear out of focus, or packed with the type of smeary motion blurs that make an image look as if it's moving very quickly.

Of course, you can easily achieve blurry or soft focus effects by simply de-focusing your lens. Why would you ever want to shoot an image in soft focus? Sometimes, you might want soft focus to create an abstract or stylized image, but the most common use for soft focus is when shooting portraits.

If you spend much time watching old movies, you're probably used to seeing certain female film stars shot through diffusing materials. The advantage of a diffuse, or soft focus effect, when shooting a portrait is that flesh tones look much better. Blemishes, pores, and other "irregularities" are blurred out to create smooth flesh tones.

Of course, the problem with simply defocusing your lens is that many details that *should* be out of focus—eyes, hair, eyelashes—will go soft. Consequently, a better way to go is to use a special diffusion filter, which you can fit over your camera's lens. Diffusion filters such as the Hoya Duto, the Cokin Sunsoft, or the B+W Soft Focus 1 filter soften bright areas in an image without reducing details, making for skin tones that are silky smooth. Using these filters for your portrait work can save you a lot of time that you would normally spend blurring and sharpening your images in Photoshop.

Of course, if you shoot with a diffusion filter, then your images will be permanently softened. It will be hard—and most likely impossible—to eliminate the effects of a diffusion filter in post-production. That's why it's important to shoot some additional frames *without* the diffusion filter. The undiffused images will give you the option of performing softening and diffusion by hand in Photoshop, if you need it. However, you'll probably find that shooting with a diffuser gives you all of the softening you need—without sacrificing the critical sharpness that you want in your fine details.

Capturing Motion

Capturing motion is a special effect that can be done in-camera by using an exposure time that's the right length or duration to allow the subject to blur sufficiently (**Figure 5.1**). This effect can also be created in Photoshop or a combination of both camera exposure and Photoshop. If you can accomplish this special effect in-camera, though, you're done in one step: the click of your shutter.

Figure 5.1 *This stop-action photograph was taken at F/5.6 at $^1/_{1,250}$ second. To convey a feeling of motion, I found elements in the scene that suggested movement, such as the shape and direction of the track. A longer exposure might better convey movement, but much of the detail within the scene would be lost.*

Figure 5.2 *This image gives us the feeling that the car and driver are moving at great speed. But, in reality, the vehicle is sitting still in the pit lane. The sensation of movement was accomplished with the use of Photoshop's Motion Blur filter in select regions of the image.*

However, if you couple Photoshop's tools and filters with a careful blending of layers, you can create a very sophisticated illusion of motion (**Figure 5.2**).

Combine any of these tools with a telephoto lens or a wide aperture, and the resulting image may exaggerate the sensation of movement. Another technique, dragging the shutter with a second curtain flash, can also give a sense of motion. (*Dragging the shutter* means using an extended exposure time with a flash synched at the end of the shutter exposure.) This kind of camera work is difficult to emulate in Photoshop. Combine any of the above with Photoshop, though, and the special effects can be either enhanced or exaggerated.

The key to in-camera blurring is your shutter speed control. Slower shutter speeds will make for blurrier images. When the shutter is open longer, the elements in your scene have time to move and smear within the frame. The easiest way to get a slower shutter speed is to switch your camera to shutter priority mode. In shutter priority mode, you can select a shutter speed and your camera will automatically choose a corresponding aperture that will yield a good exposure. Of course, a full manual mode will let you choose a slow shutter speed, but you'll be on your own to find a corresponding aperture, although your camera's light meter will tell you when you've found an aperture that yields a correct exposure (**Figure 5.3**).

While a slow shutter speed will render moving subjects blurry, it will also reveal any handheld shake. So, you'll want to hold the camera as steady as possible.

Creating motion blur in-camera also lets you easily do something that can be very difficult to do in Photoshop. If you use a slow shutter speed and, while shooting, pan your camera to follow a moving subject, then you'll have a subject that's fairly sharp and a background that's completely smeared and blurry. Creating such an effect in Photoshop would require lots of complex masking and multiple blurs.

Figure 5.3 Using a slower shutter time ($^1/_{80}$ seconds) and smaller aperture (f/22) illustrates the dramatic speed at which this car is traveling.

Controlling Depth of Field

The depth-of-field in an image refers to how much of the image is in focus, from nearest to the farthest subjects that appear sharp. Shallow depth of field is often used for portraits—or any other type of subject where you want the background to remain soft to bring attention to your foreground elements. You can achieve a shallower depth of field by choosing to use a wider aperture, and a lens with a longer focal length.

Aperture priority mode is the easiest way to tell your camera to shoot with a wider aperture. Remember, an aperture setting with a lower number yields a wider aperture, and thus less depth of field. Manual mode will also let you select a wide aperture.

Your depth of field will also get shallower as your lens focal length increases. So, to get less depth of field, stand farther away from your subject and zoom in with your lens. Then, switch to aperture priority and dial in a big aperture.

Improving Saturation

If you spend a lot of time using Photoshop to boost the saturation in your images, you'll be glad to hear that you can perform some saturation boosting when you shoot. Obviously, the easiest way to do this is to dial up the Saturation setting in your camera (if it has one). If your camera doesn't have one, or if you don't like the effects of the in-camera Saturation adjustment, *or* if you'd rather not make such a broad global change, you can alter saturation on a shot-by-shot basis by simply choosing to underexpose. (Photo journalists who seek veracity in their images usually steer clear of such enhancements.) Just be careful to not go too far, as underexposed images can lose important shadow detail.

Using your Exposure Compensation control, dial in a very slight underexposure—usually -1/3 or -1/2 stop will do. Your image will appear slightly darker, but for outdoor shots (and most other well-lit shots) this shouldn't be a problem (**Figure 5.4**).

If you're in low light, this may not be an option, both because your image will become too dark, and because an underexposure will run the risk of putting you into a shutter speed that's unsuitable for hand-holding the camera thus introducing shakiness.

Figure 5.4 Underexposing an image slightly can have some dramatic effects on both the brightness range and color.

The easiest way to learn what this effect looks like is to try it. Shoot a few images at the recommended metering, and then shoot the same shots underexposed. Take the whole batch into Photoshop, and look at the difference in the color tone in your images. At the same time, check to see if the shadows are properly exposed. You'll probably find that the underexposed images are slightly more saturated, and a little richer. Deeper color, and not a single trip to the Hue/Saturation dialog box!

Sharpening Images

When you shoot in JPEG mode, digital cameras automatically sharpen images. This default sharpening is just part of the digital camera experience. But many cameras also provide another level of sharpening that you can turn on or off. These digital camera automatic sharpeners do a very adequate job. Plus, the process is usually nondestructive—in other words, the image is not hurt in the process—and you'll still have many options at your disposal later, in Photoshop.

An image with no applied in-camera sharpening may need to be sharpened in Photoshop or with a Photoshop plug-in third-party application such as Nik Sharpener or PixelGenius's PhotoKit Sharpener. This method lets you control the sharpening-to-noise ratio separately within that particular image. Similarly, this process allows you to sharpen every image to suit a particular output, like the type of printer you plan to use.

Summary

These in-camera techniques should help you lessen your reliance on Photoshop. The results might be better than what you can achieve in Photoshop. At the very least, photographs captured with these camera tricks will give a better foundation when you do take your images into Photoshop.

Processing Raw Images

6

AT ONE TIME, TIFF and JPEG files dominated the digital landscape. Eight-bit color was the maximum we could work with in our computers. Nowadays, we have many more options at our disposal. One of the most powerful is the option to capture raw images, which contain all the information our cameras have received, and thus allow for maximum flexibility in Photoshop. Taking advantage of raw capture means developing a workflow that takes you deep into the inner capabilities of your camera and of Photoshop.

Photo credit: Jess Suworoff and Sarah Weeden

Raw images do put an extra step into our workflow. Before we can work on them, raw images must be converted into a format that Photoshop can open and read. That means raw files must be converted to an RGB color space such as sRGB, Adobe RGB, ColorMatch RGB, or ProPhoto RGB. This conversion takes place with a piece of software called a *raw converter*. Several kinds of raw converters are available. If your camera takes raw images, it probably came with its own raw conversion software. This chapter deals mainly with one raw converter in particular, Photoshop's Camera Raw published by Adobe.

Any raw converter will create Photoshop-friendly files, but Camera Raw, as part of the Photoshop package, allows you to work in Photoshop the entire way through. It's also more powerful, in some respects, than most of the other converters out there, as I'll explain later in the chapter.

After reading this chapter and orienting yourself to Camera Raw, you will know how to harness the power and flexibility of the raw image.

Getting to Know Adobe Camera Raw

Digital camera manufacturers know their technology better than any software company, but they keep secret the recipe for how their cameras' imagers and firmware perform. As a result, several camera manufacturers design and build their own raw converters to process their camera data.

Does it matter which raw converter you use? I recommend different converters for different photographic workflows. If, for instance, you are working with a computer connected to your camera (in a tethered system, as described in Chapter 3, "Seeing Your Pictures in Advance"), you should use the raw converter available from your camera manufacturer. Digital camera manufacturers design raw conversion software that can communicate both with their cameras and your computer. When you're working in a connected or tethered system, this means that any raw images you take will automatically be converted and show up on your computer. Once they're there, it's a quick step to import those images into Photoshop. In a connected system, your own camera's raw conversion software is the fastest and easiest way to go.

If you aren't working in a tethered system, and you plan to move your images manually from your camera's memory card to a computer hard drive, then Camera Raw is, in my opinion, the best choice (**Figure 6.1**). That's the scenario I'll be describing in this chapter.

Camera Raw updates

Each new version of Camera Raw brings significant improvements and features. As new digital cameras come to market, Adobe develops upgrades to address those cameras' particular raw formulas. The Adobe Web site (www.adobe.com) should be a regular stop for every Photoshop user; that's where you'll find Camera Raw updates for both Macintosh and Windows users. You can also reach Adobe's updates in Camera Raw itself, under Help > Updates (**Figure 6.2**). This chapter was written based on Camera Raw 3.3, but the steps I describe should remain accurate for subsequent upgrades (**Figure 6.3**).

Figure 6.1 The Camera Raw interface

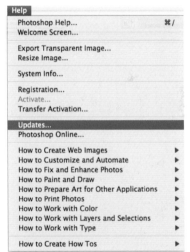

Figure 6.2 Camera Raw updates are available from www.adobe.com or under Help > Updates. Check frequently for the latest version.

Figure 6.3 This chapter uses version 3.3, but the steps should be the same no matter which version you're using.

Camera Raw setup and preferences

As with Photoshop, it's important that you set up your Camera Raw software correctly before getting to work on your images. Addressing these setup issues early on will save you a lot of time and effort in the long run.

When you open your first image in Camera Raw, it appears on the screen with some automatic features available. Auto Adjustment, for example, is handy if you're in a hurry to get a lot of toning done expeditiously. This feature automatically sets the white balance, tint, exposure, shadows, brightness, contrast, and saturation—and it does a pretty good job most of the time.

If you'd rather adjust your raw images manually, you can toggle Auto Adjustment on and off by pressing Command+U (Mac) or Ctrl+U (Windows) or through the Camera Raw menu on the right side of the screen (**Figure 6.4**). You can save your manual

Figure 6.4 Camera Raw's Auto Adjustment feature is helpful when you're in a hurry to fix your image's white balance, exposure, and other adjustments found in the Settings menu.

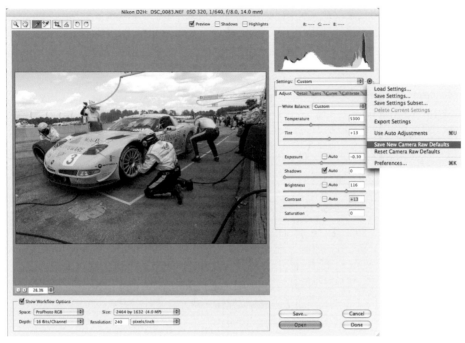

Figure 6.5 *At any point in the Camera Raw workflow, you can save your own personal Camera Raw defaults.*

adjustments to the Camera Raw menu by choosing Save New Camera Raw Defaults (**Figure 6.5**). Once you've done that, Camera Raw will offer you the same settings on every image you open, as long as Auto Adjustment mode is turned off. Take a few minutes to familiarize yourself with this little menu.

One preference you'll want to look into relates to how Camera Raw records the changes you make to an image. Camera Raw treats raw images as digital negatives; it doesn't alter the original raw file in any shape or form. Since there are well over 100 different kinds of raw files floating around these days, of which the vast majority are undocumented—encoded by the manufacturer of the particular camera that captured it—Camera Raw treats each as a read-only file (see sidebar, "Undocumented Raw File Formats"). Essentially, the original raw file will stay the same, no matter how many changes you apply to it. Instead of changing the actual image, Camera Raw uses either Sidecar XMP files or the Camera Raw

UNDOCUMENTED RAW FILE FORMATS

Many camera manufacturers keep the description of their raw file recipe unrevealed, resulting in what are called "undocumented" raw files. The information contained within a file describes how a camera and its imager capture and record raw data, and camera manufacturers consider this proprietary information.

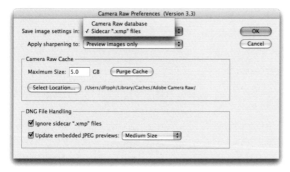

Figure 6.6 Camera Raw's preferences let you choose between Sidecar XMP files or the Camera Raw Database. Depending on how you handle your files, either may be best for you.

Database to record any changes you make to an image. This choice can be made in Preferences > Save Image Settings (**Figure 6.6**).

If you choose Camera Raw Database, these settings will be saved in the folder you select. This is a good choice if you prefer a hands-off approach to managing your files, but it means that the settings aren't portable—they'll only work when you open the image on that particular computer. Sidecar XMP files, on the other hand, create separate, portable files that can be moved fairly easily along with your raw images. The Sidecar .xmp option saves your settings in the same folder as your raw files, which enables you to move images from one computer to another (something many of us do routinely) and keep your image settings simply by moving your XMP files along with the raw images.

Figure 6.7 The Adobe DNG Converter (available for download at www.adobe.com) is a great way to simplify your workflow in Adobe Creative Suite products. It eliminates the issues associated with both Camera Raw Database and Sidecar files.

There's a third way to save your changes, and it's more flexible than either Sidecar files or the Camera Raw Database. Simply use the Adobe DNG Converter to convert your raw files to the DNG file format (see sidebar, "DNG File Format") (**Figure 6.7**). DNG files can be opened up in Photoshop directly, and they will automatically open with the adjustments you've made to them in Camera Raw, as those adjustments have been built into the DNG file substructure. You'll still be able to undo any of those changes, since you made them in Camera Raw.

Note that converting to a DNG format does not change your raw files.

DNG FILE FORMAT

DNG (short for *digital negative*) was developed by Adobe to help cope with the archiving issues associated with undocumented raw file formats. DNG is an open and documented file format, and thus more flexible in its use. DNG files can also contain end-user, or manually added, metadata.

Working in Camera Raw

Photoshop, Camera Raw, and Adobe Bridge—a photo management application we'll discuss in detail in Chapter 8, "Working in Photoshop"—are connected at the hip. If you're working with these three tools (as opposed to, say, using a third-party raw converter), your workflow will probably go like this: Bridge > Camera Raw > Photoshop. Bridge is the most logical way to surf folders of images after a photo session. If I shoot raw—as I do 95 percent of the time—my first steps after the shoot are to import those images on to my computer, and then use Bridge to cull the images I don't want. Once that selection process is complete, I click on a raw image in Bridge and Camera Raw is launched to open up my selected image. Camera Raw is where my toning and color work begins.

TIP

Remember, this process applies to a traditional, shoot-and-download workflow, *not* a tethered system. If you're using a tethered system, you'll use the raw converter made by your camera manufacturer, then import those images into Photoshop.

Workflow options

Once Camera Raw opens your image, find the Show Workflow Options menu in the lower-left corner of the main Camera Raw window (**Figure 6.8**). Setting the Space option to ProPhoto RGB gives you the maximum color your camera can capture; it allows Camera Raw to handle all the raw data that comes its way. Be warned, however, that this setting has its challenges. Some photographers report tone breaks and posterization as a result of using ProPhoto RGB.

The Size option lets you consider how your image will be used and at what magnification you'd like to see it. I usually select the default image size, which is the way the image comes in from my camera. If I need to resize the image, I'll do that later in Photoshop.

Figure 6.8 Camera Raw's Workflow Options area is the place to begin your work. It's located at the bottom left of the main window.

The next choice, Depth, sets the bit-depth or the quantity of brightness levels in my image. Raw images contain, in theory, up to 16 bits of information, that is, 65,536 levels of brightness for every channel: red, green, and blue. JPEG images, by contrast, only contain 8 bits of information per channel. If I made perfect adjustments in Camera

Raw every time, it would be unnecessary to import my images into Photoshop at 16 bits. I could import them at 8 bits, knowing I had all the information I needed. But if I need to make additional tonal adjustments (such as levels, curves, selective color) in Photoshop, having a 16-bit image is an insurance policy against posterization (which is the consequence of not having enough information to work with as you make your adjustments).

Finally, the Resolution option lets you choose the number of pixels per inch that your file will contain when it's imported to Photoshop. This is not a critical decision at this point, because you can make the same changes in Photoshop's Image Size dialog box. If, however, you plan to import several images from the same shoot and use the images in the same way, take this opportunity to choose your resolution in Camera Raw. It'll save you from having to make resolution changes on each image individually later in Photoshop. (Camera Raw's Filmstrip mode allows you to make changes to several images at once. We'll talk more about Filmstrip mode later in this chapter.)

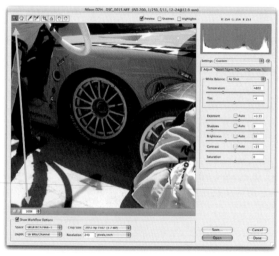

Figure 6.9 There are two ways to zoom in on your image in Camera Raw: Select Zoom Level at the lower left your screen, or click the Zoom tool at the upper left.

Zoom level

Immediately above Show Workflow Options is the Select Zoom Level dialog box. This is one of two Preview Control options in Camera Raw that dictate how your images will appear when you open them in Camera Raw (**Figure 6.9**). By default, your image will open in Camera Raw sized to Fit in View so the window is filled with your picture. This is great for looking at overall picture composition and addressing tones, white balance, color, and so forth, but I find it useful to pop the image view up to 100 percent magnification and inspect it for sharpness and detail. You can also do this (as you would in Photoshop) by double-clicking on the Zoom tool in the top-left corner of the Camera Raw window. This is even faster than using the Select Zoom Level options. You can undo your zoom by double-clicking on the Hand tool. This brings you right back to Fit in View size.

The Tools palette

At the top of your Camera Raw window is the Tools palette. I use some of these tools almost every time I open Camera Raw. The most important is the White Balance tool. This is extremely useful if your image has a light gray or diffuse highlight region that you can use as a basis for setting your white balance and tint by clicking the White Balance eyedropper on that region (**Figure 6.10**). Use caution here: If you use the eyedropper on an area of the image that is not neutral, Camera Raw will usually produce unsatisfactory white balance results. If this happens to you, visit the Settings menu and set the white balance to As Shot. This will set Camera Raw back to the original camera settings—back to the camera's white balance setting at the time of capture—and permit you to begin your work anew.

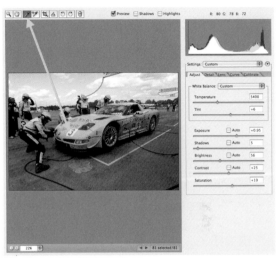

Figure 6.10 If you have a good, diffuse white or light gray area within the scene, click the White Balance tool on that area. I recommend including a white reference target in a test shot to guarantee good white balance no matter what your shooting conditions.

Immediately to the right of the White Balance tool is the Color Sampler tool, which lets you sample the RGB values within an image. With these samplers you can monitor a numerical readout of the shadows, highlights, and neutral regions of the photograph. It's also a very helpful tool to use with the test targets and charts described in Chapter 7, "Managing Color."

Moving to the right of the Color Sampler tool you will see the Cropping tool. I suggest waiting until you get into Photoshop before you crop an image; at that point, you'll have a better idea of what kind of cropping you need. This tool can help you straighten your image relative to vertical or horizontal references within the scene. Finally, the Tools palette is completed with clockwise and counterclockwise Rotate Image tools.

Preview, shadows, and highlights

Look just to the right of the Tools palette. You will see three boxes labeled Preview, Shadows, and Highlights. Preview lets you

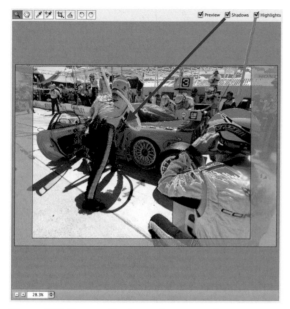

Figure 6.11 *Camera Raw's previews are a fast way to check exposure on your highlights and shadows.*

quickly toggle between before and after views of your adjustments. You'll probably find that once you try the Preview option, you'll be hooked. Immediately to the right are the Shadows and Highlights preview buttons, which allow you to turn on clipping displays shown in your camera's histogram (**Figure 6.11**). Clipping occurs when information runs out on either end of the brightness range—shadows or highlights. You can access clipping information even faster from your keyboard by pressing O for overexposure (to check the shadows) or U for underexposure (to check the highlights) to find out whether you've underexposed the shadows or overexposed the highlights. Note that the color space you have assigned in the Workflow Options section will have a dramatic effect on the amount of clipping incurred. The larger color spaces, such as Pro-Photo RGB, will show very little clipping compared to the smaller ones such as sRGB.

The Settings area

The Settings area is also where you'll find the heavy-hitter controls for making white balance, brightness, and color adjustments (**Figure 6.12**). The work you do here can potentially save you lots of time in Photoshop. That's because white balance, brightness, and color adjustments made in Camera Raw are nondestructive—unless you use Photoshop's Adjustment Layers such adjustments will make a permanent change to your image. Still, in order to make these adjustments confidently, you'll need a calibrated and profiled display, as described in Chapter 7, "Managing Color." You'll also want to use the Color Sampler

Figure 6.12 *The White Balance and Tint tools, as well as the rest of the sliders and graphs under the five tabs (Exposure, Shadows, Brightness, Contrast, Saturation) make up the business end of Camera Raw.*

tool for detail verification in your highlights and shadows—that is, to ensure that both regions of the photograph have all the information you want.

Understanding RGB readouts

At top of the screen is the RGB readout. If you are looking at your image magnified at 100 percent of its actual size—and this is usually the best way to be looking at your images—the RGB readout will give you a reading based on each 5-pixel-by-5-pixel square you move your cursor over. Camera Raw will base its reading on an average of the colors in that 25-pixel square area. This readout is activated anytime you drag your mouse over the image, regardless of the tool currently in use. It's similar to the Info palette in Photoshop, but with fewer functions.

Immediately below the RGB readout is a six-color histogram that maps out the red, green, and blue channels of the converted raw image (see "Decoding your Histogram" to decipher these colors). If you see any of those six colors in the histogram, you know that some clipping—some truncation of your image's color—is occurring. Keep in mind that some clipping is inevitable; the goal is to minimize it as much as possible.

Below the histogram, you'll see a pull-down menu for accessing the Camera Raw default settings or the raw file settings from your camera (**Figure 6.13**). When you make adjustments in the Settings area, you build new custom settings, which will stay with your image, no matter which format (Sidecar XMP, Raw Database, or DNG file) you chose earlier.

Figure 6.13 These are the master settings for your image. When you make changes in Camera Raw, you reset your image settings to Custom.

Camera Raw image controls

The five tabs available to you in the Camera Raw image controls are Adjust, Detail, Lens, Curve, and Calibrate. You can access them by clicking on the tabs, or by hitting Command+Option (Mac) or Ctrl+Alt (Windows) along with the 1, 2, 3, 4, or 5 key.

The Adjust tab contains options for setting and tweaking white balance, toning (exposure compensation, brightness, contrast), and color balancing and preferences. It is probably the most used control area in Camera Raw, and for good reason. The majority of the work you do to prepare an image for Photoshop will take place with this control function. The better a job you do here, the less time you will need to address the same issues in Photoshop. It's best to work your way from top to bottom of this window, adjusting your values to get optimal tone and color combination.

Generally speaking, if you want to play on the safe side, it's better to overexpose than to underexpose your raw captures, although you should never overexpose by more than a half stop or so. The data your digital camera captures overwhelmingly represents the highlight region of the image; only a very small part of that information represents the shadows. (If you want to go higher—expose by a full stop or two—know that your camera's histogram will indicate clipping before it occurs.) If you underexpose your raw images and then attempt to compensate for this by adjusting the shadows with Camera Raw's Exposure slider, you risk getting a significant amount of noise and less-than-optimum color in the those regions.

The Detail tab is your opportunity to adjust for sharpness and noise reduction. The sharpening tool in Camera Raw is really designed to facilitate batch processing of images. It's not intended to be a full-featured image sharpener. I strongly suggest that you go to Camera Raw's Preferences and set Apply Sharpening to Preview Images Only. In this setting, Camera Raw will not apply sharpening to the images you eventually send to Photoshop. Photoshop does a far superior job of sharpening with either its Unsharp Mask tool or the Smart Sharpener in its Filters menu. Camera Raw's Noise Reduction feature, also in the Detail tab, is not something you'll need unless you are shooting with a camera that creates a lot of noise or unless you're making exposures with high ISOs. The Luminance Smoothing slider attempts to reduce luminance noise—the bright, speckled patterns that can appear in shadows or in low-light images. It works well, but must be used

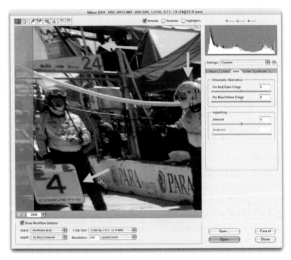

Figure 6.14a This image contains areas of color fringing, which need to be addressed with the Lens Chromatic Aberration sliders in the Settings menu.

Figure 6.14b The color fringing problem has disappeared, thanks to adjustments with the Red/Cyan and Blue/Yellow sliders set at –39 and –20, respectively.

with great caution; it will smooth important photographic detail away, along with unwanted image noise.

The Lens tab brings you to your adjustment window for Chromatic Aberration and Vignetting. Chromatic aberration, or fringing, is a problem that occurs when a lens doesn't focus the red, green, and blue wavelengths to the same point on the camera's solid-state sensor. Color fringing can also be caused by individual pixels on your camera's sensor "overflowing" and spilling into neighboring pixels. This control provides sliders to compensate for red/cyan and blue/yellow fringes (**Figure 6.14**).

Vignetting is when brightness falls off from the center of the image toward the edges. Using a wide-angle lens or a larger f/stop can exacerbate this problem. Lens vignetting can be addressed by using the Vignetting sliders (Amount and Midpoint) to smooth the illumination across the frame. The Amount slider affects how dark the dark areas of the image will be; the Midpont slider affects where the darkness begins. There is no magic formula for how these sliders should be set; most photographers will want to experiment to find the right combination. However, once you find a set of vignetting

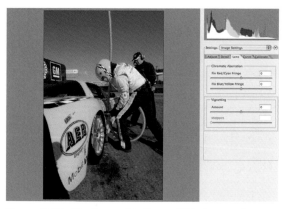

Figure 6.15a *The top and bottom of this image show darkening from its center to the edges of the image.*

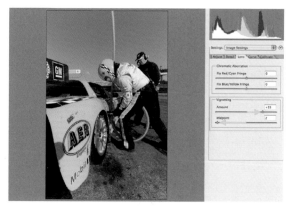

Figure 6.15b *The vignetting almost disappears as the Vignetting Amount slider value is moved to a +55, and the Midpoint slider value is moved to a +2.*

parameters that work for a particular lens, you'll probably discover that those parameters work properly with any other images shot with that lens. In addition to checking for vignetting visually, you can use your RGB readout to evaluate the changes you make with these sliders. The RGB readouts can be used like light meters, to tell you where your image is getting darker and by how much. With a little practice, you can balance your scene to the point that lens vignetting is nearly undetectable (**Figure 6.15**).

The Curve tab in Camera Raw is essentially a combination of settings available on the Adjust tab, with an important difference: changes made with this tool alters the image data, especially in the three-quarter tones and shadow areas so it's best to make small, incremental changes. Curve is great for making minor adjustments to an image's tonality, but should not be used for making major tone adjustments as you would with the Adjust sliders (**Figure 6.16**).

The Calibrate tab lets you make color-centric adjustments based on test targets such as the GretagMacbeth ColorCheckers used to make digital camera profiles. You can save these adjustments and then apply them to subsequent images. Because not every camera comes out of the factory with exactly the same color response, you can use the Calibrate tab to build a custom color calibration profile for your specific unit. This profile is not to be used as part

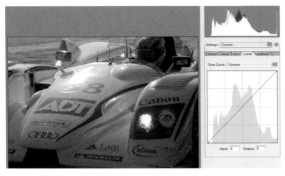
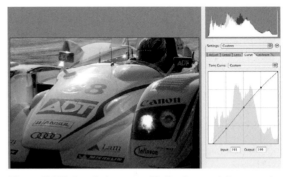

Figure 6.16a After all the major white balance tonal changes are completed under the Adjust tab in the Settings menu, you may need to make some very small changes under the Curves tab.

Figure 6.16b Small changes with the Curves tab can make a nice tweak to the contrast in an area of the image.

of your computer's color management system. It's used only in Camera Raw. Under the Calibrate tab, adjust each of the three primary colors (red/green/blue) as well as your image's gray balance. The most difficult thing to grasp is that the color sliders for a single color adjust the *other* two adjacent colors. Negative slider adjustments move the hue angle in a counterclockwise direction and positive slider adjustments move the hue angle in a clockwise direction. Both negative and positive slider adjustment on the red hue slider will actually move the green and blue hues, not the red.

You can also use the Calibrate tab to fine tune your color, but if you're just getting to know Camera Raw, you might want to save Calibrate for later for a couple of reasons. First, the adjustments you make here will not be reliable if you haven't calibrated your monitor (see Chapter 7, "Managing Color"). Second, a full understanding of the Calibrate tool requires some knowledge of color theory. Getting a handle on the Calibrate tab will take some practice, a little patience, and a lot of observation, but it's a great tool for fine-tuning your images (**Figure 6.17**).

In terms of color management, the best sources of information I've seen are *Real World Color Management*, by Bruce Fraser, Chris Murphy, and Fred Bunting, and another of Fraser's books, *Real World Camera Raw with Adobe Photoshop CS2* (both published by Peachpit Press). Fraser's procedure for Camera Raw's Calibrate

Figure 6.17a This image has not been adjusted by any of the controls in Camera Raw. If you look at the Calibrate tab, you'll see that everything is set at "0."

Figure 6.17b This image has had a positive Red slider adjustment. Notice how the reds in the histogram have remained the same, but the other colors have changed.

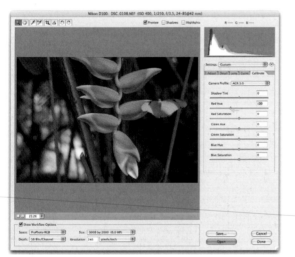

Figure 6.17c This image has had a negative Red slider adjustment. Notice how the reds in the histogram have remained the same again, but the other colors have changed.

Figure 6.17d This illustration compares the histograms from the three versions of the image. Two of the images have had Red slider adjustments—one positive and one negative. Notice how the reds stay the same, but the other colors within the histogram change.

tab is to start by photographing a 24-patch GretagMacbeth Color-Checker and then compare and adjust it to a digital version of that chart, converted to the ProPhoto RGB workspace. This target, the Macbeth ColorChecker ProPhoto RGB, can be downloaded from www.colorremedies.com. The outline that follows is an abbreviated version of Fraser's process.

USING ADJUST AND CALIBRATE WITH COLOR TARGETS

1. Illuminate your GretagMacbeth ColorChecker evenly in preparation for making a target capture photograph.

2. Using the ColorChecker's white patch as your target, adjust the exposure until your RGB reading (found in Photoshop's Info palette) is within 237–245. This is easy in a studio, but feasible on location as well. If no computer is handy, make an exposure series with the RGB settings above and below your metered reading.

3. Make a raw photograph, or a series of photographs, at different exposures.

4. Open the Macbeth ColorChecker ProPhoto RGB in Photoshop.

5. Open your test image in Camera Raw.

6. Using the Adjust tab's tone controls, match the brightness, or luminance values, of the reference image to your target capture photograph. Using the RGB numbers provided on the reference image as your guide, adjust the tone controls to approximate these values on your test image. You may find it helpful to use the Color Sampler tool to evaluate each of the gray patches as well as the red, green, and blue patches (**Figure 6.18**).

Figure 6.18 A little friend helps me hold this Mini ColorChecker as I snap his picture. Later, back at the computer, I used the Adjust tone control sliders to adjust the image to match the gray patch values on the Macbeth ColorChecker ProPhoto RGB.

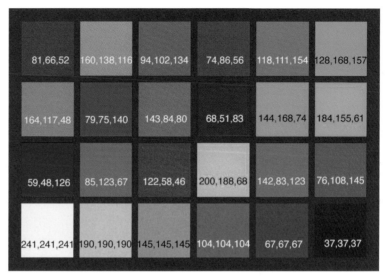

81,66,52	160,138,116	94,102,134	74,86,56	118,111,154	128,168,157
164,117,48	79,75,140	143,84,80	68,51,83	144,168,74	184,155,61
59,48,126	85,123,67	122,58,46	200,188,68	142,83,123	76,108,145
241,241,241	190,190,190	145,145,145	104,104,104	67,67,67	37,37,37

Figure 6.19 The Macbeth ColorChecker ProPhoto RGB gives the reference values to match both your gray patches and red, green, and blue patches.

Figure 6.20 Using Camera Raw's Settings controls, adjust your test capture photograph to the values identified by the Macbeth ColorChecker ProPhoto RGB.

7. Using the Calibrate tab's Shadow Tint, Hue, and Saturation sliders, match the red, green, and blue patches on your target capture photograph to the Macbeth ColorChecker ProPhoto RGB. Try to keep the relationship between the values the same, even though values may differ slightly from those listed on the chart (**Figure 6.19**).

8. Once you've made a close match between your target photograph and the Macbeth Color-Checker ProPhoto RGB, choose Save New Camera Raw Defaults as a new setting in the Camera Raw Defaults menu. Notice that the new default settings render images that are much closer to the original scene (**Figure 6.20**).

Camera Raw Filmstrip Mode

If you open a folder of raw files and double-click on an image, it will open in Camera Raw, where you can make a host of changes to that individual image. But that's like buying groceries one item at a time—it's fine in some instances, but it's a slow and inefficient way to get what you need. If you are working on a group of images that all need the same white balance, tint exposure, brightness, contrast, and saturation adjustments, your best route is to use Camera Raw's Filmstrip mode. I love Camera Raw, but I'd rather be behind the camera than the computer monitor. The Filmstrip mode helps me toward that goal to apply changes to multiple images at once.

Working in Filmstrip mode

1. Highlight two or more raw images in either the Adobe Bridge or Photoshop finder, and select File > Open in Camera Raw (**Figure 6.21**).

Figure 6.21

2. Notice that, suddenly, the separation between Bridge and Camera Raw disappears, and it's as if you are using one application only. (However, you'll no longer see the images' metadata.) You now have the ability to both preview selected images within a file and work on any selected image within the filmstrip in Camera Raw.

3. As you scroll through the filmstrip of thumbnail images, each image you select will instantly appear in the Preview window.

4. Select and highlight a group of images by Shift-clicking to add images and Command-clicking (Mac) or Ctrl-clicking (Windows) to subtract them.

5. Use the arrow keys to preview your selected images in the Preview window of Camera Raw. (Note: If you make any adjustments to an image, your highlighting will disappear and you'll have to reselect the images.)

6. Adjust one of the images in Camera Raw's Image Preview window until you are pleased with the results.

7. Locate the Synchronize button in the upper-left corner of the screen in Filmstrip view, and click once to perform all those adjustments on the selected image or all the images in the filmstrip (**Figure 6.22**).

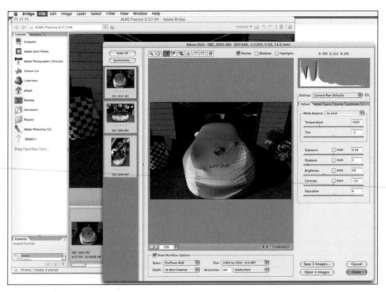

Figure 6.22

A Few Tips for Using Camera Raw

As with Photoshop, there are many ways to use Camera Raw, and each of us will approach these tasks a little differently. As a general rule, however, you can do a few things to take full advantage of this software:

- Become fully familiar with Camera Raw's adjustments, menus, toolbox, and preferences.

- Organize and rate your images in Adobe Bridge prior to importing them into Camera Raw.

- Set your Preferences for optimum productivity.

- Consider converting all your raw images to Adobe's DNG file format to avoid having to use the Camera Raw Database or Sidecar files.

- Use the Color Sampler tool to check detail in highlights, middle-tones, and shadows.

- Get to know the Camera Raw Image Controls, and use them to their fullest.

- Use Filmstrip mode for jobs that require making the same adjustments to more than one image at a time.

Summary

If you do things right in Camera Raw, you make your work in Photoshop a whole lot easier. Camera Raw, when used effectively, can minimize the devastating effects of poor judgment calls made in Photoshop. That's because the raw image captured by your camera gives you thousands of levels of brightness in every color. By the time you finish working in Photoshop to get that image to a final print, you've whittled those levels of brightness down to several hundred or less. The adjustments you make in Photoshop plays a major part in what gets discarded. Do things right in Camera Raw, and your Photoshop results should be greatly improved.

Managing Color

7

EVERY PHOTOGRAPHER AIMS to make his or her photography better, easier, and more efficient. One of the most important steps toward doing that is understanding how our equipment interprets a scene's color. This information lets us know how we're doing at the moment of capture, but it is also invaluable later, in Photoshop, when it comes time to make adjustments. Your color management process should ensure that your images' colors stay as consistent as possible throughout your workflow, but unfortunately it's rarely so easy. When you consider how many variables we face with color, it almost seems that getting it right can only happen by accident.

What do we mean when we say color management? Simply put, color management is what it sounds like: managing color in a systematic way so that you don't have to deal with it on a picture-by-picture basis. It's an attempt to keep color consistent from what we see in the viewfinder to the final print.

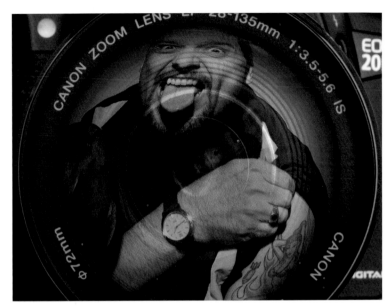

Photo Credit: Jeremy Lips

Before digital cameras, computers, and electronic printers, color management was tangible in most respects. Films were designed and manufactured with a specific color balance, letting us choose between daylight and tungsten-balanced products. Today, professional photography relies less and less on the traditional techniques like fast film processing services, contact sheets, proof sheets, and those formerly ubiquitous ink-jet prints to assess the color of their photographs. Instead, photographers view and soft-proof their images on computer monitors. One way to establish a color baseline is to use targets, charts, and color samples that let you calibrate your equipment to an established set of color values.

The Role of Targets and Charts

The word "target" generally refers to an image that can be used to test your camera's resolution, determining how sharp your lines are, for instance, and what kinds of detail you're able to capture. However, a target can also be a single color card, which is used to determine white balance, color, or tone reproduction. "Chart" usually refers to an arrangement of whites, grays, or colors—anywhere from two to 200 variations on color and light—used for the same purpose. These terms are often confused, or even used interchangeably. I'll use "target" as a general term for an object placed in an image to test an aspect of that image.

Targets, charts, and white balance

White balance simply means adjusting your camera, or image in the computer, to the color of the light source in a photograph—setting a color bias. Photographers often achieve acceptable white balance without test targets, but targets can ensure that things are working correctly the first and every time. Targets can really go the distance when it comes to setting a good white balance. Sunsets, snow scenes, portraits—all require different white balance settings, and targets can help show us which one to choose.

There are three basic ways of achieving a good white balance using the charts and tools listed below. All of them will work, although options 1 and 2 are preferable to option 3. In all three methods, begin by placing a reflective chart—like one of those pictured in **Figures 7.1** through **7.6**—in front of your camera, making sure that your primary light source will strike it evenly.

Figure 7.1 The GretagMacbeth Color Checker White Balance Card is a large and spectrally neutral reference. It's also fast and easy to use. It may, however, prove difficult to use in some very brightly lit scenes.

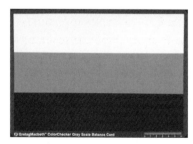

Figure 7.2 The GretagMacbeth Color Checker Grayscale Balance Card can help set white balance and a mid-tone gray value that you can use later for color-correcting in Camera Raw, Lightroom, or Photoshop.

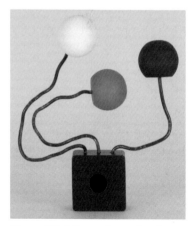

Figure 7.3 A three-dimensional reference like Megavision's ToneBalls can be excellent for setting white balance, because the photographer can see how light hits the subject from different angles.

Figure 7.4 A WhiBal is a rugged, pocket-sized, and spectrally flat— a neutral gray color. They can be used to set white balance in almost any level of light.

Figure 7.5 Sometimes you don't want a true white balance. WarmCards are helpful when you want to give your photographs a warm quality—for instance in portraiture.

Figure 7.6 ExpoDisc filters—used for setting custom white balance—come in both white balance and warm balance models. First, place the disc in front of the lens and point the camera at the light source. Then, use your camera's Custom White Balance option to make a custom setting. (Just make sure that your ExpoDiscs are big enough in diameter to cover your largest lens.)

Figure 7.7 In Adobe Camera RAW, simply click on your chart with the White Balance tool. Here, I'm using a WhiBal Reference Card. The chart does not have to be in focus, but it must be illuminated by the dominant light source.

THREE WAYS TO SET WHITE BALANCE

1. Cameras with the custom white balance feature: Fill the camera's viewfinder with the chart and then select the Custom White Balance option in the camera menu. When you capture the image, the camera will adjust its white balance and maintain those settings for the images you capture under those lighting conditions. (Exception: See ExpoDisc instructions under Figure 7.5.)

2. Cameras with the raw capture feature: Make a good exposure of your scene including the reflective chart. Remove the chart and shoot. After you've transferred your images to the computer, open them in your raw converter, select the White Balance option, and then click on the test chart in your image. The converter will establish the correct white balance and allow you to save and apply those settings to all the images with those lighting conditions (**Figure 7.7**).

3. Cameras with the JPEG-only capture feature: Make a good exposure of your scene including the reflective chart. Remove the chart and resume making photographs. After you've transferred your images to the computer, compare the image with the chart and adjust it until the image shows the chart to be neutral in color. For example, if the chart is too red, adjust your color until the image appears balanced. The easiest way to do this is by going to the Photoshop menu and choosing Layer > New Adjustment Layer > Color Balance, Levels or Curves mode. Those settings can be saved and applied to other images that were made under the same lighting conditions.

Tone and color charts

Tone and color reproduction are exactly what they sound like: the processes of creating tones and colors that are faithful to the scene as the photographer saw it, or to his or her specific intention. These targets can also be used for digital camera color management.

To use one of the charts pictured in **Figures 7.8** through **7.10**, simply include it in a test shot prior to a photo session. (These targets can also be used as a tool for setting white balance, as described in options 2 and 3, earlier. So in practice they serve two purposes.)

Figure 7.8 The Macbeth ColorChecker is the industry standard for color evaluations.

Figure 7.9 The Macbeth Mini ColorChecker is a 2 ¼-inch by 3 ¼-inch version of the Macbeth ColorChecker.

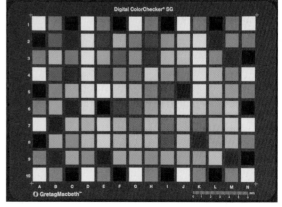

Figure 7.10 The Macbeth ColorChecker SG consists of 140 semigloss color and grayscale swatches. It's used for full-color assessment and can help build digital camera color profiles.

Ten Steps for Effective Testing with Targets

1. The camera lens must be perpendicular to the target, in other words, on a 90-degree angle with the test target (**Figure 7.11**).

2. Targets should be placed at an appropriate distance from the lens, depending on guidelines set by the target manufacturer.

3. Lights must be set at a 45-degree angle to the test target as in Figure 7.11.

4. Take care to light the target very evenly. A handheld meter, set in incident mode, will ensure an even light distribution. There should be no more light deviation than a $1/10$ f/stop or less at any point on the target (**Figure 7.12**).

5. Place your camera on the sturdiest camera support you own.

6. Use a shutter release cable (remote trigger release) if possible. If you don't have one, put the camera on self-timer mode.

7. Be absolutely sure that your lens elements are clean and free of dust and fingerprints.

8. Make sure that your camera's sensor is clean of surface dirt. Check your manufacturer's camera manual for cleaning instructions.

Figure 7.11 The test target is at a 90-degree angle with the digital camera. The lighting is at a 45-degree angle on each side of the camera. The camera is mounted on a sturdy tripod with a Lindahl Professional lens shade installed at the front of the lens. This setup can be arranged with a tape measure and spirit level.

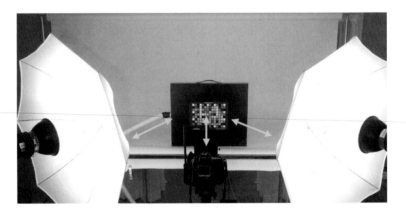

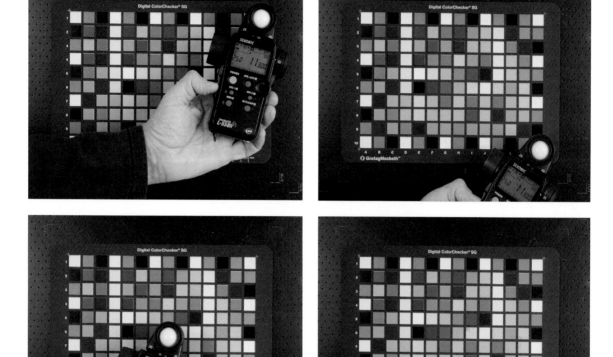

Figure 7.12 *Using a light meter, measure light levels across the test target. Adjust lighting so that the reading is the same, no matter where on the chart you hold the meter.*

9. No extraneous light should strike the front lens element. A professional lens shade, or compendium, is a sure way to reduce or totally eliminate this problem.

10. Measure and take note of your entire test parameters. This will allow you to repeat the test later, if necessary (**Figure 7.13**).

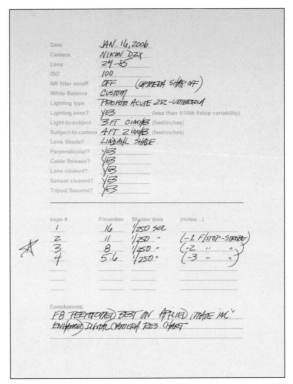

Figure 7.13 A good record of your testing procedure and data is an invaluable reference for making a final assessment of your camera and lens performance. Plus, it keeps you organized during the testing procedure.

If you take just a few moments to prepare your testing procedure, use the right tools, and record your test results for later reference, you will get some very useful information about how your camera is performing.

Reviewing test results in Photoshop

After conducting a tone and color test, you'll be eager to see the results. There's no better place to do that than in Photoshop. These 10 steps take you through that process.

1. Make sure your monitor is calibrated. We'll discuss display calibration later in this chapter.

2. Open Photoshop and toggle to Full Screen Mode with Menus by using either Photoshop's Toolbox or pressing Command+F (Mac) or Alt+F (Windows) (**Figure 7.14**).

3. Open the first test image (**Figure 7.15**).

4. Press Command+R (Mac) or Alt+R (Windows) to make Photoshop's rulers visible. Drag out horizontal and vertical guidelines from the horizontal and vertical ruler bars. These will show you whether your target is squared up proportionally in the viewing area (**Figure 7.16**).

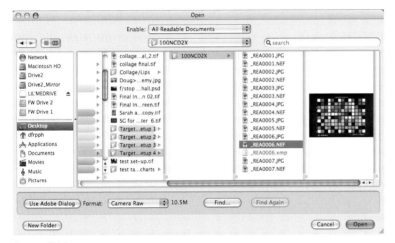

Figure 7.14

Figure 7.15

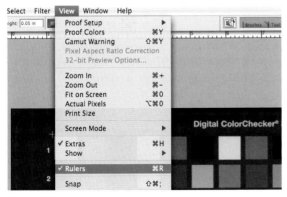

Figure 7.16

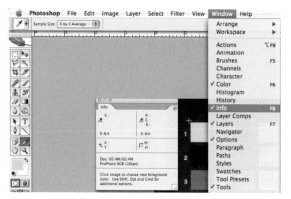

Figure 7.17

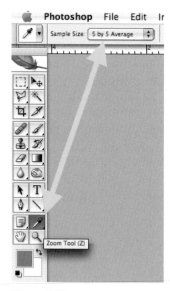

Figure 7.18

5. Press F8 to reveal Photoshop's Info dialog box, then read selected areas of the test target to see if your lighting is even. Strive for a brightness level change of less than 10 levels across the target. Gray cards are best for determining the evenness of your light (**Figure 7.17**).

6. To evaluate the distribution of grays in your image, open Photoshop's Eyedropper tool, either by clicking on the Eyedropper in the Photoshop Toolbox or by pressing Command+I (Mac) or Alt+I (Windows). Change the Sample Size from the default Point Sample to 5 x 5 Average. This will give you a 25-pixel Eyedropper—ideal for many photographic readings of test targets (**Figure 7.18**).

7. Use your Info tool to see if selected regions of your test target are neutral, meaning gray, or without any color bias (**Figure 7.19**).

8. Evaluate your image at 100 percent. Engage the Zoom tool by pressing Z (in Mac or Windows). Then select the Actual Pixels radio button in the Options bar. Select Photoshop's Hand tool and then hold down the spacebar to move the target around the computer's display. This will help you navigate the image to see if it has gray balance or image noise problems.

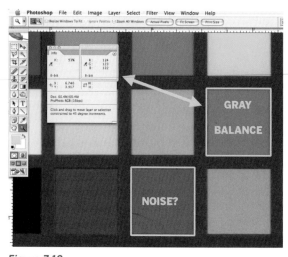

Figure 7.19

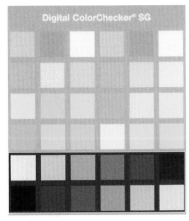

Figure 7.20

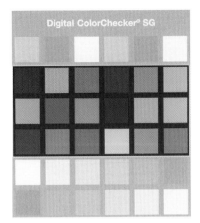

Figure 7.21

9. Evaluate your tone reproduction by comparing grayscales and color swatches to your actual test target(s) (**Figures 7.20** and **7.21**).

10. Open up other test target shots (from different camera settings or with different lenses) in Photoshop and compare the results in the same way as outlined here.

Understanding Color Profiles

Charts and targets, as I've said, can play an important role in color managing your digital camera workflow. We use them to establish a baseline for color that we can now use to calibrate our equipment. Let's look at what color profiles do and how they are applied.

A digital camera gives us many, many choices for how to use it, and sometimes, that's exactly the problem. Changes that seem inconsequential at the time we make them can have a significant impact on color relationships downstream. The ability to change your ISO, for example, is a wonderful thing when you need to photograph in unusually light or dark environments, but it can also affect the color in your image. Changing lenses can also affect color, as will exposure errors, long exposure times, and the quality of light in your scene. One of the most important challenges in digital camera color management is maintaining a consistent color temperature of lighting.

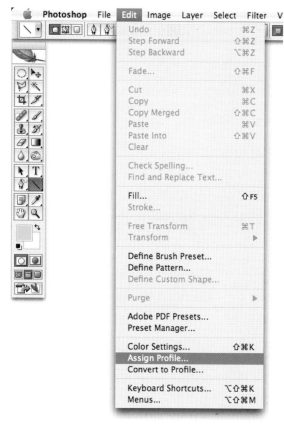

Figure 7.22 *You can see your range of available color profiles by choosing Photoshop > Edit > Assign Profile. In the resulting dialog box, you can either assign a profile that is provided by the camera manufacturer, assign your own custom profile, or use the Working RGB color space.*

The color you see in your digital images depends on what's called a "color space," a particular range of colors within which the image is displayed. The most common color spaces are sRGB or Adobe RGB, but raw capture gives you access to more options, like ProPhoto RGB and Color-Match RGB (**Figure 7.22**). These color spaces—or profiles—describe the entire color gamut of an image, regardless of whether that image contains all those colors. Some color spaces are broader than others and, generally speaking, broader is always better.

If I know that the lighting in my photographic scene is stable (for example, in a studio), I will often build a custom profile for my digital camera. It takes only a few minutes behind the camera and at the computer to get the job done, and it makes for fewer adjustments later in Photoshop. A custom profile ensures that your computer will interpret the colors of an image correctly, according to the specific qualities of light in that particular scene, and the way your camera captures it. Other times, when I know my lighting conditions can change in a heartbeat, building a custom profile is a waste; instead I use the camera's built-in settings. Then I can do color management later when I'm sitting in front of Photoshop. It all depends on your style of photography and the conditions under which you work.

Camera profiles provided by camera makers

Most digital cameras produced today come with one or more of the following color profile options:

■ An embedded profile—usually the default factory setting is an sRGB profile.

- A choice of profiles—generally sRGB and Adobe RGB.

- No profile—for cameras with raw capture capability.

If you are capturing in JPEG mode, accept the opportunity to override a camera manufacturer's sRGB preset and choose Adobe RGB if it's offered. Adobe RGB is a significantly larger color space than sRGB (**Figure 7.23**).

If your camera gives you the option of shooting raw files—to capture images without having to attach either the sRGB or Adobe RGB color spaces—that's even better. Raw images provide all the color information a camera can capture. Later, when you move your raw images to Adobe Bridge, Lightroom, or Photoshop, you'll assign a color profile anyway. At that point, I always choose the ProPhoto RGB profile, simply because it guarantees me the largest mapping of color available today—much better than anything I can get in JPEG mode. Raw images allow you the most flexibility in terms of color management, especially in those situations where building a custom digital camera profile is either impractical or impossible.

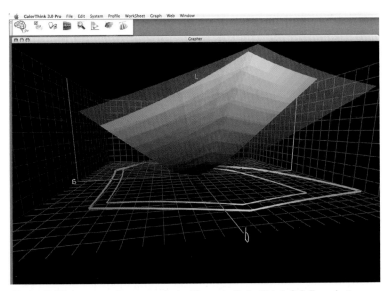

Figure 7.23 A comparison—made in Chromix ColorThink 3.0 Pro—between two profiles. This is a graphic example of two color gamuts, or ranges of color. The smaller opaque graphic is the sRGB gamut. The larger color transparent graphic is the Adobe RGB gamut.

TIP

Keep the target flat! It's important that you keep your test targets and color charts away from humidity, sunlight, or excessive heat that might warp them. Warped cards are more difficult to light and frame evenly during a test procedure, and images from warped cards are also a pain to handle in the profiling software. When your targets or cards are not in use, store each in its protective sleeve, and keep them in a dry and cool place. If your card warps, store it under some pressure to flatten it for its next use. I often place my cards under some heavy books to ensure that they'll be flat next time I need them.

Custom color profiles

If your camera and lighting do not change over the course of a photographic assignment, then you should profile your digital camera before the first shot is made. It may take the first-time user some time and practice to complete the process, but 15 minutes or less will do the trick. But even in stable conditions, you may still want to build additional profiles. Here are a few of those scenarios:

- The type of lighting may change, for example, from one set of strobes to another, or from strobes to hot lights or tungsten lamps.

- The camera's ISO may need resetting.

- You may need extended shutter times to capture ambient lighting in addition to the primary light source, such as a strobe.

- Your shoot involves colored gels or colored reflector cards.

- You want the freedom to modify your lighting reflectors or modifiers by, for example, switching from umbrellas to softboxes.

In all of these cases, your camera's ability to capture color will change. Every time you introduce a new variable, you must build a new profile to keep your color consistent.

Building a Digital Camera Profile

Building a custom color profile requires a colorimeter, a combination of hardware and software built for that purpose. Colorimeters can run up to $2,000, although some are much more affordable. Know that you can't mix and match technologies from different manufacturers. For instance, if you're using a GretagMacbeth Colorimeter system, you won't want to introduce elements from an X-Rite Colorimeter system. The colorimeter hardware you purchase will not be upgradable, although software generally is. It's a good idea to visit a manufacturer's Web site frequently to see whether upgrades are available.

Color management companies sometimes introduce newer charts too, which can provide better color sampling and gamut mapping than their predecessors. A good example is the evolution of the GretagMacbeth ColorChecker target to the GretagMacbeth ColorChecker DC and, ultimately, to the target that many color specialists use today, the GretagMacbeth ColorChecker SG. Each upgrade gives us the opportunity to capture and produce more refined color. No system is perfect, but color management keeps getting better and better.

The steps below are based on an X-Rite Pulse ColorElite system, though you can also use the GretagMacbeth Eye-One Match. In addition to this software, I use a GretagMacbeth ColorChecker SG as a target.

Getting started

1. If you haven't already, install your profiling software onto your computer.

2. Consider connecting your computer to your camera with a tethered system, as described in Chapter 3. It's a much faster way to get at your test shots than the "sneaker net" approach. If you're unable to hook your camera up to your computer, your best alternative is to have easy access to a laptop, to which you can move images frequently and quickly. I often keep my laptop close at hand so that I can run back with my memory card, download a test image, and build a quick profile based on what I see on the monitor. This lets me inspect my camera's exposure and evenness of lighting across the chart, something you can't do with a camera alone.

3. Place your color test target, or chart, in such a position that you're able to center it within the camera's viewfinder. I like to fill the finder with the chart if possible. I use my camera view-finder's frame lines to ensure that the camera is perpendicular to the test chart. In fact, the frame lines are a more accurate measure than the perimeter of your viewfinder (**Figure 7.24**).

4. If you're in the studio, place your lights at a 45-degree angle to the target. Adjust the lights so that lighting is perfectly even across the chart. I use a handheld light meter to deter-mine this. I also often use a professional lens shade to ensure ethat extraneous light doesn't affect the profiling procedure. If you're working on location under available lighting that can't be controlled, locate and place the target in a place where it is lit as closely as possible to the subject of the image. At all costs, avoid hot spots and shadows, as they will ruin the test procedure. Trust me, I've done it.

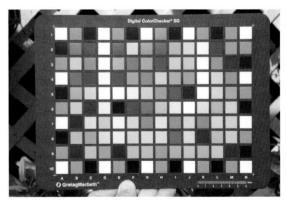

Figure 7.24 Holding a chart perpendicular to the camera is tricky at times, but it can be done if you're careful to frame it squarely within the viewfinder. Also it's essential that the lighting be even across the target.

5. Set your camera's white balance on a neutral part of the card or on another chart that is neutral. If your camera permits, make a custom white balance. (Note: Every camera manufacturer that includes this feature does it a little differently. Check your owner's manual to find the manufacturer's procedure.) Some Nikon cameras, for instance, give you the option of putting the white balance in what's referred to as a "PRE mode." You then fill your frame with the neutral part of the card and press the exposure button. No picture is made, but the camera evaluates the white balance and allows you to save it as a custom white balance setting. Alternately, if you have a color meter, determine the Kelvin temperature reading, and apply this K value in your camera's white balance setup menu.

6. Continue to adjust the lights as you make a few test shots. If you are in a tethered PC environment, adjust the lighting and exposure until the white patches on your chart give average RGB readings between 210 and 245 in Photoshop's Info palette (Window > Info, or the F8 function key). Make sure that brightness levels don't vary any more than 10 units between sampled white patches across the chart (**Figure 7.25**). If you don't achieve even lighting, this profiling procedure will ultimately fail.

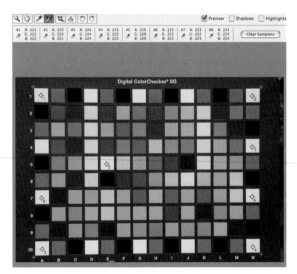

Figure 7.25 This is a cropped view of a chart in Camera Raw. Note that the color samplers at the top of the image referring to each of the white patches across the chart (8 samples taken) all have almost the same reading. This proves there's equal lighting and appropriate exposure for this environment. This should be your goal.

7. Once your lighting and exposure are even across the target, make your test shot. If you have a connected PC, you'll be able to check and inspect your results almost immediately in Photoshop. If your PC is nearby, that'll work, too. But if you're unable to get to your PC, you should make several different exposures of the test chart in a variety of lighting situations to ensure that you get a usable image to profile. This is especially important if you're shooting JPEG or TIFF files.

8. As long as your lighting conditions are constant, you can venture on to making photographs of your subjects. If the type of lighting changes, make another test shot as outlined in steps 4 through 6.

9. After you return to your computer with your test shots and assignment photos, launch your profiling software (**Figure 7.26**).

10. Your profiling software will walk you through the process. The first thing you will be asked to do is load a photograph of your test chart image (**Figure 7.27**). Then carefully follow the rest of the instructions given by your system's manufacturer.

11. After you've finished the process, you'll be prompted to save your profile in the appropriate folder on your computer. Once you've done that, you've built a profile for your digital camera (**Figure 7.28**).

Did profiling make a difference?

The only way to find out whether this color profiling process is worth your time and effort is to give it a try. After you've built a profile for a particular photographic scene and lighting, open several of your images in Photoshop CS2. Depending on your camera settings and how the images were imported, these images will be set at sRGB, Adobe RGB, ColorMatch RGB, or ProPhoto RGB.

Figure 7.26

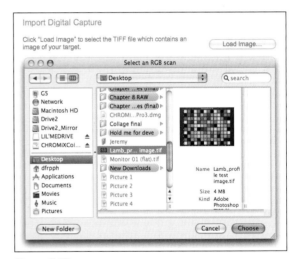

Figure 7.27

Figure 7.28

Select at least one of these images and proceed with the following:

1. Assign your camera's new custom profile in Photoshop to a sample image made under the same lighting (**Figure 7.29**).

2. Use the preview button to look at both before and after views of the image (**Figure 7.30**).

3. If you can, compare the monitor's image with your original scene. This is easy to do in the studio, but more difficult on location shoots. (It's also another argument for a connected PC, which allows you to make this comparison almost instantaneously.)

4. Having assigned your new profile to an image, check to see whether the new image looks closer to what you shot than what you got using the generic profile. If it does, then you have a winner.

Figure 7.29

Figure 7.30

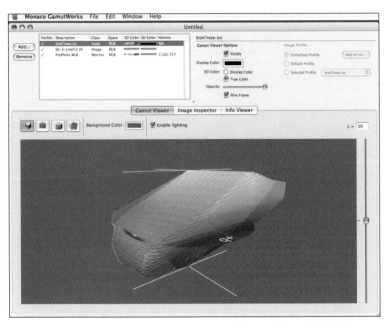

Figure 7.31 Both Chromix ColorThink Pro and Monaco GamutWorks let you compare your profiles as either 2-D or 3-D graphics. These graphics can also be rotated on-axis, providing a 360-degree view of your color gamut. (This image was generated in Monaco GamutWorks.)

TIP

Map that gamut! Two really neat tools to help you visualize how your color profiles compare are Chromix ColorThink Pro and Monaco GamutWorks. Both applications provide a variety of graphics and tool sets to help you see how your color gamuts compare (**Figure 7.31**).

Now that your camera is profiled, let's take it one more step. When you look at your monitor to see how your custom-profiled image compares to a color-managed image in Photoshop, how do you know the comparison itself is accurate? That sounds like a circular question, but the answer is straightforward: You need to profile your monitor. According to your workflow, it may very well be the first step of the color-management process.

Profiling Your Display

As with your camera, profiling your monitor requires an expensive colorimeter but less-expensive display color calibrators can also be used. A display calibrator—a hardware/software combo used exclusively for getting accurate color adjustments on computer display—will run you about $200, while a colorimeter may cost five times that. This chapter is based on using the GretagMacbeth Eye-One,

WHAT IS A DISPLAY PROFILE?

A display profile is a file of attributes that describe how a monitor (or other device) reproduces color. These attributes include information about the device's white point, brightness and contrast, gamma, and, of course, color.

Most photographers use display calibrators or colorimeters to set the right profile for their display. A proper display profile helps ensures accurate color conversion from the display to another device, such as a printer.

WHAT IS CALIBRATION?

Calibration is the process of making a device color-neutral—kind of like setting your scale to zero. When you calibrate your display, you take steps to ensure that it does not have a color bias. Displays must be calibrated, but so must the calibrating device. Your calibration software will walk you through this process.

a very popular color management tool, but with display calibration, the process is going to be roughly the same no matter which device you choose.

Thankfully, the color management software you use will walk you through the process of creating a custom profile for your monitor (**Figures 7.32** and **7.33**).

Like anything else, monitors age, and the way they display color will change over time, so you'll need to repeat the profiling process periodically, maybe once a month. Unless you work in different locations, you probably look at your display in the same room with the same lighting, so you'll also want to set up the best possible viewing environment.

The combination of a calibrated display and consistent viewing conditions ensures that the image on your monitor looks the same as your subsequent soft proof; you'll have continuity throughout the process, and no surprises.

Figure 7.32 This LCD display is set at its default display profile, the Apple Cinema Display settings. You'll find this option in System Preferences > Displays > Color.

Figure 7.33 This LCD display is set at a custom-generated profile. (Inset portrait courtesy of Greg Gorman)

SHOPPING FOR A DISPLAY?

Choosing the right display is not always a slam-dunk. You can't just shop brand, size, and price and hope the color comes out right. You need a monitor that yields even and consistent brightness, contrast, and color. Find a display that provides both excellent peak brightness and black level.

Here's a simple test you can do in Photoshop: Create an empty window with a white background. If the white background doesn't fill the screen, use the zoom tool until it does. Toggle this empty window to full screen mode and press the Tab key to hide Photoshop's tools. In front of you will be a totally white screen. Inspect the display for unevenness in color and brightness. Look at the display from different angles—move from one side of the display to the other to see if there are any inconsistencies in its brightness or color. If you note any big changes, this is not the display for you. (Once you're done, press the F key to return to standard screen mode.)

Ten steps to a profiled display

1. Thoroughly clean your display with a cleaning cloth and display-safe cleaning solution.

2. Turn lighting in the room off or to a very low level. Make certain that no ambient room light is hitting the display surface.

3. Launch your profiling software, and follow the instructions to select your white point (I recommend 6,500k, or D65 as it's sometimes called), gamma (I recommend a gamma of 2.2 for any computer), and luminance. Follow the on-screen recommendations for laptops and LCD panels or use the on-screen tools to help you establish the best brightness and contrast settings for a CRT display (**Figure 7.34**).

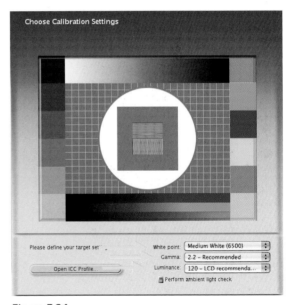

Figure 7.34

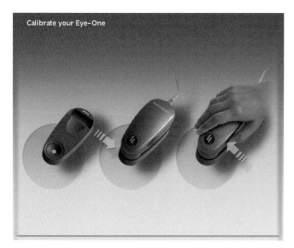

Figure 7.35

Figure 7.36

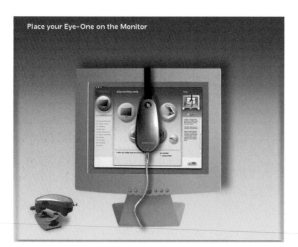

Figure 7.37

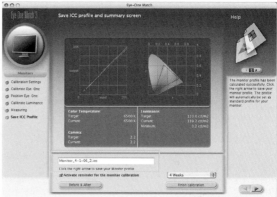

Figure 7.38

4. Begin the profiling process of calibrating your measuring device according to the manufacturer's instructions. This ensures that your readings will be accurate (**Figure 7.35**).

5. Place the measuring device on your display (**Figure 7.36**).

6. Follow the steps your profiling software walks you through to determine what brightness and contrast settings you should use. I suggest that you follow the recommendations that the software makes for your display type (**Figure 7.37**).

7. You may also find it necessary to adjust the brightness of the lamp you use for print viewing (this could also be a print viewing booth—see "Ten steps to the right viewing environment" in the next section) to match the intensity of your display.

8. Following the software's instructions, go through the process of building a profile for your display.

9. Name and save your display profile by choosing Library > ColorSync > Profiles (Mac) or Windows > System32 > Spool > Drivers > Color (Windows) (**Figure 7.38**).

10. Repeat this process every one to four weeks.

WORKING BY THE NUMBERS

If you're out in the field, or for some other reason can't be sure that your display is giving you accurate color representation, there's one more option. Working by the numbers means learning how to interpret the K (grayscale), RGB (red, green, blue), and CMYK (cyan, magenta, yellow, black) values in Photoshop's Info palette. Print reproduction professionals use these numbers routinely, but they can be a bit daunting for the uninitiated.

The K value is a percentage of how much black ink will be placed on the page when this image is printed. RGB values represent levels of brightness with 0 equaling black and 255 equaling white. CMYK values—like the K value—indicate the percentage of cyan, magenta, yellow, and black ink that will be printed on the page.

First, you'll need to make a good print from a reference image. Then open the image in Photoshop and explore that image's highlights and shadows by moving your cursor over it and reading the feedback in the Info palette. Note what the corresponding K, CMYK, and RGB values are on your computer's image (**Figure 7.39**). These numbers will provide a reference for evaluating future printed images to see if they contain sufficient shadow and highlight information.

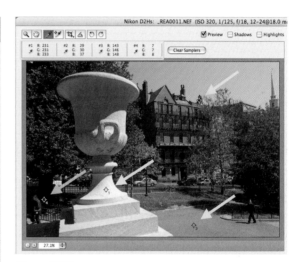

Figure 7.39

The Right Viewing Environment

Profiling your display is important, but so is setting up the right viewing conditions. If you're working on location—as photojournalists often do—it's next to impossible to establish a good viewing environment. In these cases, you must rely on your laptop and its profiled display. (For another option, see the sidebar "Working by the Numbers.")

In the office or studio, however, it's a whole different ballgame. You should set up your environment and computer display so that it is neutral in tone, contrast, and color. Follow the instructions in this section to set up your space (**Figure 7.40**).

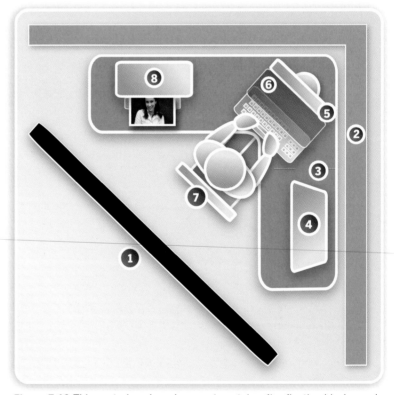

Figure 7.40 This neutral work environment contains: 1) a floating black panel; 2) middle gray walls: 3) gray table tops; 4) a light booth with rheostat lighting control; 5) display; 6) monitor hood; 7) chair with arms at table height (approximately 30 inches); and 8) a printer. (Image credit: Kim Miller)

Ten steps to the right viewing environment

This process may seem like a lot to tackle, but it will make a world of difference when it comes time to read and evaluate your images. A profiled monitor is just one factor in seeing color accurately. Environmental conditions play a big role, and you will notice a significant difference if you follow the steps outlined here.

1. If possible, place your computer in a corner of your room.

2. Paint the wall(s) behind the computer with middle gray (18 percent gray) or light gray flat paint. Be sure that the gray is neutral without a cool or warm bias. If you're unsure, use a middle gray sample from a GretagMacbeth ColorChecker as a gray reference. You can also have the ColorChecker's gray reference matched at your local paint store.

3. Use a computer display hood to keep nearby light sources off your display.

4. Use a 5,000k to 6,500k light bulb or a viewing booth. Place it near your computer in such a manner that it doesn't throw light on your computer display. It's helpful to use a hooded viewing booth or station that's large enough to accommodate your prints. If you purchase a viewing booth, be sure to get one that has rheostat lighting control. This will allow you to vary the intensity of the light in an effort to approximate the brightness of your computer's display. (Note: These display booths are costly. If you're on a tight budget, look into a daylight-temperature desk lamp as a less expensive alternative. You can often find them in art supply stores.)

5. Work in a darkened room. Your workspace should have no direct ambient source of light striking your display or nearby reflective work surfaces areas. Close the room's window blinds, turn off overhead lighting, and remove any conventional desk lamp you might have near your computer.

6. Make sure your work surfaces are neutral and nonreflective, or flat.

7. If possible, place a large black flat behind your chair. This is simply a floating panel that can keep ambient room lighting from striking the display.

8. When working at your display, avoid wearing brightly colored clothing.

9. If you wear eyeglasses, inspect them for color tints or yellowing that comes from normal everyday use. Wear glasses with lenses that are neutral in color.

10. Arrange to have your color vision checked at an ophthalmologist's office. The Farnsworth-Munsell color discrimination test is still, to my knowledge, the best there is to determine whether you have color vision deficiencies. A color vision deficiency is something you can learn to work around. If you suspect you might be making errors in color judgments, it's worth getting your color vision checked.

Summary

The steps I've described in this chapter—using targets to assess color balance, creating custom camera profiles, and calibrating your display—all combine to ensure that colors of the world you photograph reproduces those of the world you see. If you've never worked through the phases of color management, you'll find this all a little daunting. But the best photographers I know take the time to measure and calibrate their equipment as well as set up a consistent viewing environment. It may seem tedious but it's well worth it.

Working in Photoshop

8

UP UNTIL NOW, you've done all the right things. You've set the camera's exposure, color settings, noise reduction, ISO, white balance, learned how to operate a tethered system, and manage raw files. The quality of your images will be well worth the effort, and you will find that the time you spend in Photoshop is much better spent.

The first part of this chapter is about customizing your Photoshop settings in order to create a productive and efficient digital workspace. In the second part, we'll take the first steps toward editing and optimizing your images—picking up on the work you've already done with your camera.

Configuring Photoshop

To get the most from working in Photoshop, it pays to take time to set up the software to suit your particular computer, workflow, and imaging goals. Start by defining your computer's capabilities and establishing your software preferences.

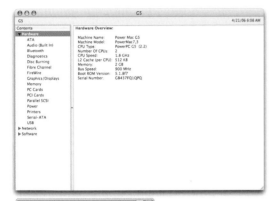

Photoshop likes computers with fast processors—the faster the better. Having *dual* fast processors in your computer is even better. If you don't know what kind of processing power you have, you can find out in your computer's About or System Information panels (**Figure 8.1**). For doing serious work on large photographs, you'll want to use a workstation or tower computer with a large screen. Laptop computers give you mobility, but they simply don't offer the processor and bus speeds that workstations do, although they are convenient for doing on-location work. If you're going to be doing a lot of photography both in and out of the studio, you may find you need both a workstation and laptop. How much RAM should your computer have? Unless you're working on small files with few layers, you should add as much RAM as you can possibly afford to both your workstation and laptop computers. RAM is cheap these days compared to a few years ago. If you have insufficient RAM, Photoshop will use what's called "scratch disk space" on your hard disk in an attempt to cover for the inadequacy in memory. The necessity to use a scratch disk instead of real RAM can actually slow down your computer, so it's best to bite the bullet and order the real thing.

Figure 8.1 It's important to know what kind of hardware you're working with. On a Macintosh, this information is under Apple > About this Mac. On Windows, see System Tasks > View System Information.

Photoshop preferences

Many important Photoshop option settings are kept in the Preferences file, including display, file saving, cursor, transparency, and options for plug-ins and scratch disks. Preference settings are saved each time you quit out of Photoshop. A large part of how your work environment will look and operate is established here.

Preferences are easy to find in Photoshop (**Figure 8.2**). On a Windows platform, hit Control-K; on a Macintosh, Command-K. If you want to use a pull down menu instead, you'll find Photoshop's preferences here: Photoshop > Preferences (Macintosh) or Edit > Preferences (Windows). The Preferences area is your launch pad, or home base, for establishing how you want Photoshop to look and act while working. You can move to any Preference window by simply hitting Command-1 through 9 on a Mac or Control-1 through 9 on Windows. Start with the General preferences and work your way through all nine dialog box categories to create your own custom settings. Although Preferences are just that—*preferences*—you can use the settings described below as a place to start then modify each as necessary for your own particular needs.

Figure 8.2 *Photoshop Preferences is where you should go when opening Photoshop for the first time, or on a new computer. The right setup here can save you lots of trouble later on.*

GENERAL

I leave most General preferences as they are, with a few exceptions (**Figure 8.3**).

When you increase or decrease the size of an image, Photoshop adds pixels to make the image larger or eliminates pixels to make it smaller. This process is called interpolation.

Bicubic interpolation looks at a large grouping of surrounding pixels within an image to decide what should be added when you increase your image size, and what should be eliminated when decreasing it. The Bicubic smoother preference allows you to make an image larger with less of an "edge effect," that is, without exacerbating noise. Bicubic sharper allows you to downsize your image without giving the appearance of lost detail within the scene. Nearest neighbor is the fastest, but poorest form of interpolation, as it

Figure 8.3 *Most General preferences can be left as they are. However, consider selecting Bicubic for Image Interpolation as a default setting.*

simply looks for the adjacent pixel information, i.e., "nearest neighbor," to fill-in for newly created pixels when the image is resized. It will give your images "jaggies" (a stair-stepping of pixels), which are really ugly.

Bilinear interpolation takes a closer and better look at surrounding pixels. It's a lot smoother than Nearest neighbor, and if we didn't have a Bicubic option, it would most certainly be the method of choice.

But I stick with Bicubic, which is the default. If I want to change the size of my image, I use the Image Size menu (Image > Image Size > Resample Image). At that point, I can select the best method for a particular image I'm working on, based on whether I will either decrease or increase the size of my image.

The General Preferences area is also where you'll find the Tool Tips option. If you're a full time user of Photoshop then you may find the Tool Tips—those little yellow boxes that tell you a tool's name as you pass the cursor over it—pretty annoying after awhile. You can turn this feature off by unchecking Show Tool Tips. I also check the Automatically Launch Bridge box since I use Bridge with Photoshop almost every time.

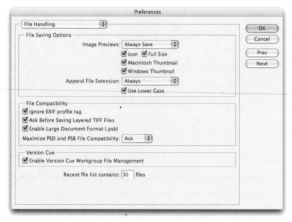

Figure 8.4 File Handling contains your options for file saving, compatibility, and versioning.

FILE HANDLING

The File Handling preference addresses how Photoshop deals with file saving, compatibility and versioning. The only thing I absolutely must change here is Recent file list contains. I increase the number in the box to the maximum permitted—30—to allow me to look back over as many recent files as possible (**Figure 8.4**).

You may also want to change the way Photoshop saves files in terms of Previews and Extensions. For instance, under Image Previews, I select the fields that indicate that an Icon or Thumbnail (whether Macintosh or Windows) will always be saved, so that regardless of where I send the image, the thumbnail or icon will always be available. And I always Append File Extension to my images so my file types are readily identified by myself or whomever handles my images at the photo lab. Other than that, I leave everything else at its default setting.

DISPLAY AND CURSORS

The Display and Cursors preferences are all about appearances, but appearances are important: they determine the look and feel of our Photoshop tools. Since I frequently use a pressure Wacom tablet and stylus (these graphic input tools allow me to do much more subtle work) in addition to my computer's mouse or touch pad, it makes sense for me to set the Paint Cursor to Full Size Brush Tip and the Other Cursors to Precise (**Figure 8.5**). You may have some special tools for which you'll modify the look of your cursors, otherwise the default settings should be fine for most users.

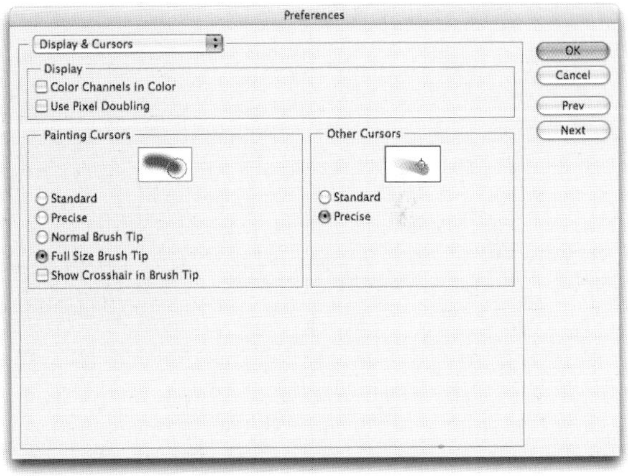

Figure 8.5 The Display and Cursors preferences are all about appearances.

TRANSPARENCY AND GAMUT

The Transparency and Gamut Warning Preferences (**Figure 8.6**) are also all about appearances, and I find that they hardly, if ever, interfere visually with my photographic scenes. Gamut Warning allows me to identify out-of-gamut colors—colors that are outside the color range my printer can produce and will therefore have to be compressed to conform to the printer's profile. You can easily identify your out-of-gamut colors by selecting Gamut Warning under the View menu. Setting this preference to 25 percent opacity makes it still possible to see a trace of the underlying image (**Figure 8.7**).

Transparency Grid Size settings change the physical size of the blocks that you see when you look

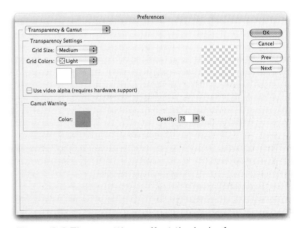

Figure 8.6 These settings affect the look of Photoshop's grids and the way the application alerts you to color problems.

Figure 8.7 Gamut Warning gives you a preview of those areas that have out-of-gamut colors within a particular color space. They do so without completely obscuring the underlying image.

at an image with a transparent background. Video alpha is used to overlay images from Photoshop into video—something I've never used and is generally not relevant to too many photographers (it also requires special hardware).

UNITS AND RULERS

The Units and Rulers preferences are helpful to photographers as they prepare images for their computer's display and, eventually, to print. Find your printer's optimal print resolution by checking your manual and set the Print Resolution to match. Find your optimal display resolution in the display manual and enter this number next to Screen Resolution (**Figure 8.8**).

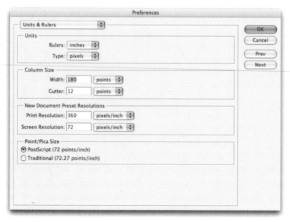

Figure 8.8 Units and Rulers preferences affect the way your images print.

Units and Rulers also let you choose column size, point/pica size, and units, but these relate to graphic design and print metrics, nothing photographers usually need on a daily basis.

GUIDES, GRID AND SLICES

Guides, Grids, and Slices are non-printing elements that help you look at your image. They're great for evaluating the composition of an image, or to see how two or more areas within an image align. To see your Guides, Grids or Slices effectively, though, you need them to be in a color that contrasts with the photograph (**Figure 8.9**). For instance, if I'm working on an image that is predominantly blue in color, I will select a highly contrasting grid color like yellow or orange. Photographs that are very gray work better with a bright colored grid, as opposed to Photoshop's default gray grid. This is even more important when working with monochrome (black and white) images, upon which it's almost impossible to see Photoshop's default gray lines. This preference also lets you customize the size of your grid.

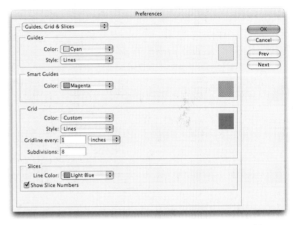

Figure 8.9 *Changing the colors of your guides, grids, and slices can make them easier to make out above your image.*

PLUG-INS AND SCRATCH DISKS

When you are running low on available memory, Photoshop will turn to a designated hard disk to borrow temporary memory. You can choose which hard disk it uses and in what order. If you have more than one internal hard drive in your computer, or if you're using an external USB2 or FireWire hard drive, it's important to sequence these drives from fastest to slowest in the Scratch Disks slots. If possible, start with a dedicated hard drive with a lot of open space and then add any additional hard drives you have available. Photoshop will begin with the first disk and move to the next one if necessary (**Figure 8.10**),

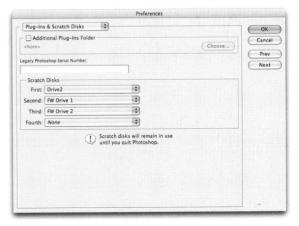

Figure 8.10 *Scratch disk space is where Photoshop finds temporary memory when your needs exceed the amount of RAM you have installed.*

using these disks as space on which to temporarily store information. This preference area also allows you to select an Additional Plug-in folder. This is a location where you can store plug-ins that you want to be able to access in Photoshop CS2.

MEMORY AND IMAGE CACHE

Memory and Cache settings affect both Photoshop and overall computer performance.

Image Cache is how Photoshop lets you preview images quickly. In other words, when image cache is active, it saves additional low-resolution versions of the image so that changing views on screen doesn't require the computer to reload the entire full-resolution image. I suggest you leave your Cache Level at 6. If you often work on larger files, a higher Cache Level will speed up the rate at which you can see the changes you make to an image. If you work with smaller images, or if you don't have much RAM, you might try working with a lower number, so as not to take processing power away from other applications on your computer. Experiment with different Cache Level settings (1 through 8) to see what works best for your particular setup (**Figure 8.11**).

Figure 8.11 Experiment with different Cache Level settings (1 through 8) to see what works best for your setup.

Figure 8.12 Efficiency information for any Memory and Cache Preference setting is updated regularly and available in the status bar.

This Preference area is also the place to indicate how much RAM can be dedicated to Photoshop. The default setting is 70 percent, but you can see how efficient your memory allocation is by checking the status bar's Efficiency option at the bottom left of the active image area (**Figure 8.12**). If you are seeing less than 100 percent in this window, you will benefit from dedicating more RAM to Photoshop and/or adding RAM to your computer. (If you don't see an efficiency percentage, click on the small triangle at the bottom of the image area and choose Efficiency from the Show menu.)

In general, it's better to have a higher percentage of memory allocated to Photoshop than to other applications, but you'll find that too high a percentage will start interfering with the performance of other software you may have operating simultaneously. I have found that I can easily increase that memory allocation to 75 or 80 percent and still reserve enough RAM for my operating system to perform its tasks without running into problems. The numbers are a bit lower on my Windows machines because of the way in which Windows handles memory allocation.

TYPE

Most photographers don't use type within their images, but for those that do, the Type preference is the place to customize it. Font Preview Size sets the way fonts are previewed in Photoshop's Option bar at the top of the screen. I set this at Small so that I can quickly review the variety of fonts on any given computer.

Photoshop allows you to use either straight quotes—those used for an abbreviation of inches or feet—or typographer's quotes—also referred to as "curly" or "smart" quotes—which blend in with the curves of the typeface.

Photoshop Color Settings

Photoshop Color Settings (Edit > Color Settings or Command-Shift-K on Mac or Control-Shift-K on Windows) is a critical setup screen for taking control of your color workflow. This is where you manage your color workspaces, color management policies, and conversion options (**Figure 8.13**). If you work in Camera Raw, I suggest you set your RGB space for ProPhoto RGB. It's the widest color workspace and it allows you to preserve the full color gamut captured by your camera. If, however, you are capturing either JPEG or TIFF files, I recommend using Adobe RGB.

Photoshop's default CMYK values are the industry standard for printing on coated paper from an offset press. The same is true for Photoshop's default 20 percent Dot Gain for both Gray values and Spot colors. Dot gain is the physical increase in the size of the halftone dot that occurs in the process of printing. Photoshop

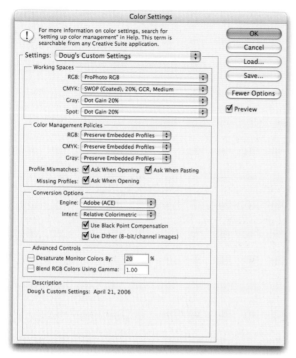

Figure 8.13 *I've found these color settings to be most effective in my work.*

takes this into account by compensating for dot gain in both the gray and spot color values of an image. Unless you are producing your own halftones and color separations (CMYK), these values won't need to be addressed. If you are, you should consult whomever is printing your images to find out how he wants to receive your files.

Under Color Management Policies, select Preserve Embedded Profiles for all three categories. This will allow you to manage color profiles on an image-by-image basis; your image's color space is preserved until you decide to change it. Also, check all the boxes next to Profile Mismatches and Missing Profiles. This will allow you to manage your files as you import and save each in Photoshop.

Click the More Options button in the main Color Settings window to reach the rest of your color settings. Under Conversion Options, select Adobe (ACE) for your Engine. Adobe conversion relies on Photoshop-centric color conversions, as opposed to working with the third-party color engines found on either the Mac or Windows platforms. The simplest definition of "conversion option" is that it's the color software that handles and converts colors from image input to display to print. Secondly, choose the Relative Colorimetric option as your Intent. This specifies how Photoshop converts colors to a printer's color space. Relative Colormetric is generally considered to be the rendering intent of choice for most photographs, and usually allows for the best match between an image's destination colors and its source colors.

I also recommend you check Black Point Compensation, which maintains the shadow detail of an image by simulating the full dynamic range (i.e. the full range of grays) of the output device. When you select the Use Dither option, Photoshop mixes colors in the destination color space to approximate a missing color that existed in the source space. Dithering helps to reduce (by smoothing or blending) the banded appearance that an image can take on when it is converted from one color space to another. Leave the rest unchecked and, of course, save your settings.

Evaluating Your Images

Everybody evaluates images differently; what's detailed below works for me. However, you'll need to pick and choose from these steps and build your own workflow.

When photographers first look at an image, we usually respond by saying, "I like it" or "I don't like it." We tend to be visual learners, which means that we start the image evaluation process by looking for what is wrong in an image or in a group of images, editing them down to identify the misses, near misses, and hits. (Metadata can be a big help in this process, as explained later in this chapter.) There are times, however, that we need to work with the near misses. In fact, just about every image has something wrong with it. Photoshop can often help us disguise, or even eliminate these flaws. Evaluating what's wrong with an image is the first step in optimizing it for a better appearance.

There are some basic techniques every photographer should apply when reviewing images. The first has to do with your initial review. As we saw when processing raw images in Chapter 6, Adobe Bridge is great for reviewing your image files. You can set it up to get a quick review of enlarged thumbnails, and then toggle to the film-strip view for a closer look (**Figure 8.14**). Bridge lets you add labels to your images to rate them according to your tastes. Bridge also lets you take a fast look at individual images for sharpness, but the lion's share of close-up image evaluation work must be done in Photoshop.

In this section, we will look at some major categories and techniques for evaluating your images in Photoshop. Not all of these techniques must be used on every image. If you shot your image correctly, you may already know that your image is virtually noise free at ISO 100 or 200, in which case checking for noise will be a relatively quick process. But even images that are shot correctly can benefit from some Photoshop help. Here's an overview of some of the most common image fixes you may encounter.

TIP

If it ain't broke don't fix it! I've often caught people carrying out adjustments that their images don't need, or, worse yet, performing adjustments that will have an adverse affect on their image. Take sharpening, for instance. Some photographers sharpen every image, whether it needs it or not—and often, that image would have looked better without it. To avoid doing something in Photoshop that's either of no value or actually damaging, always fully evaluate your image before you decide to make an adjustment.

Figure 8.14 *For evaluating images, Adobe Bridge is an indispensable tool. It provides several ways of viewing images, including thumbnail (above) and filmstrip (below)—a great combination for fast edits and evaluations.*

IMAGE NOISE

Image noise is indicated by graininess in the image, usually in areas of uniform color—blue sky is a frequent culprit. Noise can range from annoying to nasty, and if you use a high ISO on your digital camera you'll probably have significant noise to deal with.

The first step is identifying in Photoshop whether noise is a problem and how best to reduce or eliminate it. First, magnify your image to 100 percent. If you detect overall noise, look at each channel (R, G, and B) to confirm your suspicions. You can do this by opening Window > Channels and then either clicking on each channel or hitting Command-1, -2, and -3 on a Mac, or Control-1, -2, and -3 on a Windows computer. Noisy images have a grainy, coarse appearance that's especially noticeable in non-detailed areas. It's often easier to detect noise levels in separate color channels than it is to do so in a composited RGB image, since noise can be greater in one channel than others.

Photoshop gives you a very powerful means of reducing image noise without throwing out scene information or detail. Go to Filter > Noise > Reduce Noise. The dialog box that appears will give you the tools necessary to lessen the noise significantly, if not eliminate it entirely (**Figure 8.15**). I recommend that you skip the Sharpen Details part of this filter. There are better places to administer sharpening in Photoshop, as we'll soon see.

Figure 8.15 This image was captured with an ISO of 1,000. The level of noise is high, but by using Photoshop's Reduce Noise filter in the Advanced mode and adjusting the noise and detail levels on the red, green, and blue channels, we've substantially improved image quality.

ADJUSTMENT LAYERS

Adjustment layers allow you to make non-destructive edits to tone and color. You can turn the changes on and off as often as you like, until the end of the process when you "flatten" the layers, making the changes permanent. Adjustment layers also eliminate the loss of data that occurs when you make multiple tonal adjustments on the original's background layer. You can even do selective editing by painting onto an adjustment layer's image mask, in order to apply tonal or color adjustments to part of an image, such as the sky, or a face. Finally, adjustment layers from one image can be copied and pasted to other images.

Tone adjustment

Within a photographic scene, printed or on a monitor, we see a variety of levels of brightness. These are often referred to as tones, or levels of gray. It's easiest to classify them as midtones (middle grays), highlights (bright grays), and shadows (dark grays). Quarter-tones are located between the highlights and midtones (**Figure 8.16**), while three-quarter tones take place between the shadows and midtones. If the relationship between these tones is incorrect in your image—for instance, if your image is overwhelmingly composed of three-quarter tones and shadows, with few highlights or midtones—then you must make toning adjustments in Photoshop.

Figure 8.16 *This image is described in terms of tones. As you look through your camera's lens, or on your computer's display, it's important to locate the five basic tonal areas. You can then assess how to best capture and utilize these tones using your computer.*

The best way to alter tones to your liking is to use adjustment layers (**Figure 8.17**). Adjustment layers allow you to apply different tone treatments (like Levels, Curves, Brightness/Contrast, and more) to find the best combination for your image, and to get a sense of how it will look when printed. Better still, adjustment layers don't permanently change the image data—that is, until you "flatten" the image by using the Layers palette—every adjustment you make will be reversible (**Figure 8.18**).

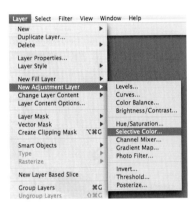

Figure 8.17 You'll find adjustment layers on Photoshop's pull-down menus, in the Layers palette, or by clicking F7 (function key 7 on Mac or Windows) on your keyboard.

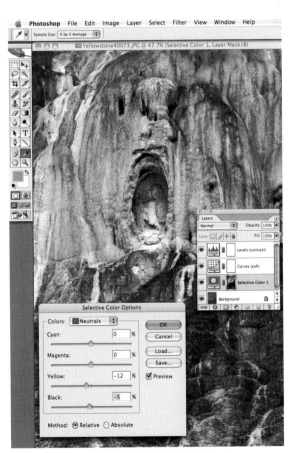

Figure 8.18 Selective Color is one of 12 adjustment layers at your fingertips. Adjustment layers can be edited or eliminated at any time without causing any harm to the background image—that is, until you flatten the image in the Layers palette.

5% (250,244,202)

95% (29,29,29)

Figure 8.19 Shadow detail can be lost if you don't watch your data points in Photoshop's Info palette.

Shadow detail

Assuming you have done whatever you can from behind the camera to maintain your image's shadow detail, it's important to keep it that way in Photoshop. Even subtle adjustments to an 8-bit JPEG image in Photoshop can crush shadow detail in a heartbeat.

Ultimately, what matters is how your shadows look when printed, so before you print your image, use your Info window (F8 or Window > Info) to check both K value (grayscale, or percentage of black) and RGB averaged values (0-255 brightness levels). As a general rule, it's good to have detailed shadows at RGB levels of at least 27. For instance, if we had an RGB reading that breaks down to a R=25, G=27, and B=29, the average of these three readings would =27. This gives us a corresponding K value of 90 percent black. Anything less puts you at risk of ending up with blackness in places you wanted to hold shadow details (**Figure 8.19**).

Highlight detail

That concern about capturing and maintaining sufficient detail applies to highlights as well. In order to make sure your highlights don't appear blown out, set a ceiling for RGB averaged values at 244, and no lower than a 5 percent K value for detailed highlights. Use your Photoshop Info window to move across the image and check the RGB readings of the highlight regions where it's essential to hold your detail. If you exceed these numbers, the subtlety you saw in your highlighted areas may be lost forever.

Color balance

A condition for good color is having your camera set at the appropriate white balance for a particular lighting environment. If you've used the right white balance, evaluating your color balance should be a lot easier and more objective (see Chapter 7, "Managing Color" for more information). If you have a test image on hand that includes a color chart, such as a GretagMacbeth ColorChecker Mini, you have a reference to consider as well (**Figure 8.20**).

With the test image open, hover your mouse over each of the color chart's squares. Use Photoshop's Info window to check the gray swatches for neutrality—that is, to make sure they are color balanced. Investigate the RGB values of each swatch to see that they are numerically very close—for example, 239, 236, 235 respectively. Once in awhile, they'll all be the same. If the RGB values are wildly skewed, you'll want to use an adjustment layer, such as Levels, Curves, Selective Color, or Color Balance to make adjustments to the test image (**Figure 8.21**). The kind of layer you select will depend on your own preferences, so it's a good idea to experiment with all of them. Once you've hit on the right setting, you can apply them to other images shot under the same lighting conditions. Here's how.

Figure 8.20 Before you start a photo assignment, be sure to include a chart in your scene to act as a color reference once you move images to Photoshop.

1. Open a test image that includes a GretagMacbeth ColorChecker Mini (as shown in Figure 8.20) within the scene.

2. Go to Layer > New Adjustment Layer.

3. Select the type of adjustment layer you'd like to use: Levels, Selective Color, Curves, or Color Balance to manipulate your color values.

4. Manipulate each color (R,G, and B) until it is extremely close, or identical, to the other two.

5. Use your Adjustment Layer's Save button to save this setting.

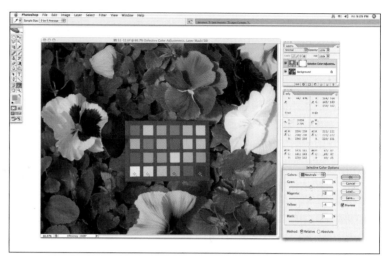

Figure 8.21 In the figure above, a Selective Color adjustment layer was created to adjust the gray values to neutral.

TIP

If you use a view camera, adjustments to the camera's sensor/film and lens planes can often be made before a shoot to prevent distortion and converging lines that occur at the time of capture. You can address distortion on your D-SLR camera by installing a PC (perspective control) lens.

6. Apply the same Adjustment Layer settings (Levels, Curves, Selective Color Option, and Channel Mixer) to other images made under the same lighting conditions. With a new image open, make a new adjustment layer of the same type by pressing the Load command. Navigate to your saved adjustment layer.

Lens distortion

Lens distortion is a problem that can result from using a wide-angle lens, or in images with converging lines, such as architectural photographs.

Luckily, Photoshop offers a Lens Correction filter (Filter > Distort > Lens Correction). The Lens tab in Camera Raw gives you some of the same tools, but in Photoshop you have even more to work with. Photoshop's Lens Correction tool set allows you to reduce pin cushioning (the kind of lens distortion you get with fish-eye lenses) and perform both vertical and horizontal perspective transforms, to adjust an image so that its converging lines are less dramatic (**Figure 8.22**). The built-in grid will also help you verify your corrections (**Figure 8.23**).

Figure 8.22 *A before and after transformation using Photoshop's Lens Corrections filter.*

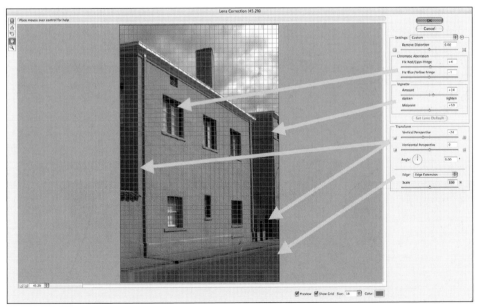

Figure 8.23 *These Lens Corrections filter settings were used to create the image on the right side of Figure 8.22.*

Sharpness

When evaluating an image for sharpness, make sure to view it at 100 percent—no exceptions. Our computer monitors can only display images at about 72 pixels per inch, which is a coarse grid of pixels compared to what we see in printed output. That means we need to get as close a view of our images as possible. Assuming that your in-camera sharpening was turned off, that your Camera Raw sharpening was in the Preview mode only (see Chapter 6, "Processing Raw Images"), and that you didn't do any sharpening with Photoshop's Reduce Noise filter, you should have a image that can be evaluated objectively and, if necessary, sharpened. If your image has already been sharpened in-camera, you'll need to be especially careful not to over-sharpen it when using a Photoshop sharpening filter.

For years many of us used the Unsharp Mask filter (Filter > Sharpen > Unsharp Mask) with varying degrees of success. Due to that tool's limitations, other third party software developers have produced their own sharpening products, such as PixelGenius's Photokit Sharpener, Nik Software's Nik Sharpener Pro, and PictureCode's NoiseNinja. Addressing the limitations of Unsharp mask, Adobe added a Smart Sharpen tool (Filter > Sharpen > Smart Sharpen) that works very well (**Figure 8.24**).

Figure 8.24 Smart Sharpen is a more refined sharpening tool than Unsharp Mask. Compare these two image areas, one before Smart Sharpening and the other after. Smart Sharpen also allows you to address your image's shadows and highlights separately.

Evaluating Images with Metadata

Assessing your image visually and getting feedback from Photoshop tools is one way to determine what edits your image requires, whether that image be a JPEG or a raw file. If you do shoot in raw mode, another open avenue is to examine the internal data that delineates how a raw image is captured and what settings were used. As we discussed in Chapter 3, "Seeing your Pictures in Advance," metadata is an important tool for reading clues about how the camera recorded the image: the ISO, aperture, white balance, and so on. Some of that data is readily accessible through readouts on your camera's LCD screen. But to understand the full extent of what metadata can tell you, you'll want to open the image in applications that can work with raw images, such as Photoshop, Bridge, Camera Raw, and Photoshop Lightroom. Raw converters from companies other than Adobe—Apple, Canon, Nikon, Olympus, and others— also read metadata.

There's a lot to discover when poking around an image's metadata, perhaps it's more information than you ever thought you needed. But intelligent analysis of metadata yields important inforamtion critical to your image editing decisions.

The different kinds of metadata

Your computer provides four major categories of metadata. Most of these information fields are fixed and can't be altered, different kinds of metadata allow levels of flexibility—some metadata can even be entered manually. To access your image's metadata in Photoshop, simply click Command+Option+Shift+I on the Mac or Ctrl+Alt+Shift+I on a PC.

- File properties. This metadata includes the most basic information about the image, akin to an image's title page. File properties include the image's name and type, the date on which it was created, its resolution information, and more (**Figure 8.25**).

Figure 8.25 Basic image information.

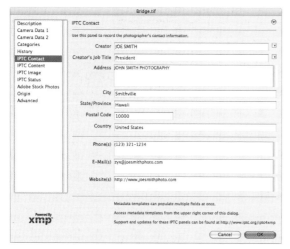

Figure 8.26 *IPTC metadata provides extensive fields for image information.*

- IPTC metadata. The IPTC (International Press Telecommunications Council) began as an information standard developed by the Newspaper Association of America to identify transmitted text and images. But it has come a long way since then. IPTC is an assortment of blank fields into which you can enter information critical to you, your client, or your editor—for instance, the image's subject, or a thematic category to which it belongs. IPTC metadata offers far more fields than you'll probably ever use and some tags, like GPS location, may not be supported by your camera. Almost all image editors read and write metadata, so IPTC information travels with the image as you move files from one location to another. These fields can be altered at any time (**Figure 8.26**).

- Camera data (EXIF, or Exchangeable Image File). Exchangeable Image File, or EXIF, is a file format used by most digital cameras, and it's the home of your image's most important metadata. EXIF was developed by the Japanese Electronics Industry Development Association in order to simplify and standardize the movement of data between imaging devices and software. Today, JPEG, TIFF, and raw images are all saved with EXIF data. EXIF metadata includes camera settings and scene information to help you understand exactly how your image was shot, including shutter speed, date and time, focal length, exposure compensation, metering pattern, flash usage, and much more. These fields cannot be altered (**Figure 8.27**).

- Raw file metadata. Whenever you make an adjustment to a raw image—such as changing the tone, color, sharpness, or white balance—those changes are recorded as metadata in a separate file called an XMP sidecar file. In essence, this sidecar metadata associated with the image contains a history of that image, detailing all the adjustments ever made to it. If you haven't made adjustments, the metadata will not appear (**Figure 8.28**).

Camera Data (Exif)	
Exposure	: (Multiple values)
Exposure Mode	: Manual
Exposure Program	: Manual
ISO Speed Ratings	: 200
Focal Length	: 80 mm
Focal Length in 35mm Film	: 120 mm
Lens	: 24.0–85.0 mm f/2.8–4.0
Max Aperture Value	: f/4.0
Software	: Ver.1.00
Artist	: Doug Rea
Date Time	: (Multiple values)
Date Time Original	: (Multiple values)
Date Time Digitized	: (Multiple values)
Flash	: Fired, strobe return light not detected
Metering Mode	: Pattern
Orientation	: Normal
Light Source	: Flash
Custom Rendered	: Normal Process
White Balance	: Manual
Digital Zoom Ratio	: 100 %
Scene Capture Type	: Standard
Gain Control	: 0
Contrast	: 1
Saturation	: 0
Sharpness	: (Multiple values)
Sensing Method	: One-chip sensor
File Source	: Digital Camera
Make	: NIKON CORPORATION
Model	: NIKON D2Hs
Serial Number	: 3003814

Figure 8.27 *EXIF metadata includes camera settings and scene information for your image, but can't be altered.*

Bridge File Edit Tools Label View Window

102ND2HS

Favorites | Metadata
► File Properties
► IPTC Core
► Camera Data (Exif)
▼ Camera Raw

Raw Filename	: _REA0096.NEF
White Balance	: Custom
Temperature	: 6150 °K
Tint	: –33
Exposure	: +0.80
Shadows	: Auto (0)
Brightness	: 86
Contrast	: Auto (0)
Saturation	: 0
Sharpness	: 25
Luminance Smoothing	: 0
Color Noise Reduction	: 35
Chromatic Aberration R/C	: 0
Chromatic Aberration B/Y	: 0
Vignette Amount	: –27
Vignette Midpoint	: 50
Shadow Tint	: 0
Red Hue	: 0
Red Saturation	: +12
Green Hue	: –33
Green Saturation	: 0
Blue Hue	: 0
Blue Saturation	: 0
Tone Curve	: Custom

Figure 8.28 *Raw file metadata details all the changes you make in an XMP sidecar file.*

TIP

EXIF Metadata can come in very handy when you're editing. For example, suppose you start editing an image and discover that the edges of the image are soft focus. You check the EXIF data and discover that your aperture is very small. Many lenses get very soft at extreme apertures. Since you now know that your image is soft and was shot with a small aperture, you can go browse your alternate images to find one with a larger aperture.

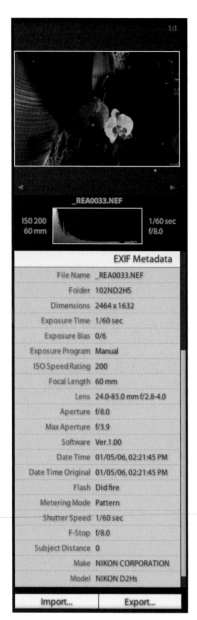

Figure 8.29 The metadata fields in Adobe Photoshop Lightroom (here shown in a beta version) are planned to be cleaner and easier to use that those in Photoshop or Adobe Camera Raw. The software was not shipping at press time.

Metadata in other applications

The raw converters in Adobe Bridge, Photoshop Lightroom (**Figure 8.29**), Photoshop, and manufacturers, raw converters such as Apple, Nikon, Canon, Olympus, and others, provide far more extensive metadata than what you will find in just about any digital camera. These programs allow you to track down almost anything you might need to know about the image. Each application, however, places metadata in a different location, which can make it a bit of a challenge to easily find the information you need (**Figure 8.30**).

Evaluating your metadata while shooting can help ensure that you don't make mistakes that will have to be corrected later in Photoshop.

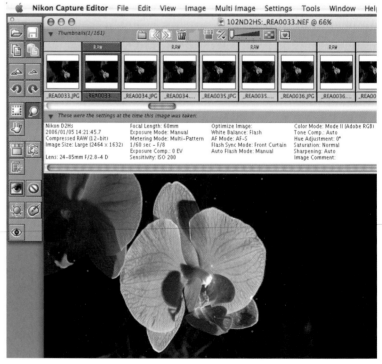

Figure 8.30 Nikon Capture (recently updated to Nikon Capture NX) has its own metadata fields located neatly between the thumbnails and the preview image.

By tapping into your camera's metadata, you get a quick review of the complex arrangement of functions and settings that created that image—and with digital cameras as complex as they are, this information is wonderful to have. Once you begin to navigate metadata, you'll discover that this information will improve your technique for future photographs, and give you a sense of what went wrong in images already captured.

Summary

Digital image editing involves visual inspection, software feedback, and metadata analysis. Sometimes just one approach will suffice, but often the best results are obtained when the three are used in combination. Image editing does take practice, however, so it's always a good idea to save variations of your images frequently or better yet, to use Photoshop's adjustment layers to experiment with color and tone corrections *ad infinitum*.

But before you get started pushing those pixels around, configure Photoshop to suit your workflow and imaging intent.

Managing Your Digital Photographs

9

BACK IN 1990 a colleague sat down with me as I demonstrated Adobe Photoshop 1.0. It was an exciting peek into the future. "At last, a civilized darkroom!" she exclaimed. She was right, of course, but at that point we worked on puny 1-megabyte files. No professional photographers took those images seriously—they were too small to even begin to approach the quality of a regular camera image. The whole process of digital photography seemed experimental and futuristic.

Now that digital photography is accepted and even encouraged in most situations, the number of images being produced has skyrocketed. No need to buy film in bulk. Just purchase a few high-capacity storage cards and re-use them over and over again. As a result, today's photographer has to manage thousands of images from a single shoot.

This chapter will introduce you to some tools and practices that you'll want to consider for managing your post-production workflow.

Editing and correcting images is only a part of the photographer's post-production chore. One of the great advantages of shooting digitally is that it's far cheaper than film technology. You can take hundreds of pictures without burning through rolls of expensive film. While this allows you a tremendous amount of creative freedom in the form of bracketing and experimentation, it also means that your post-production work is complicated by a glut of images. Sorting and organizing those images, and identifying the select images that you want to edit, correct, and output is often more of a chore than editing your images. If you're employing preventive Photoshop practices to minimize your editing, then sorting and organizing may make up the bulk of your post-production.

It makes sense then to establish a workflow that streamlines the process of reviewing and selecting your images.

Workflow Defined

Your workflow will vary from shoot to shoot and project to project, and you'll often take different approaches to your post-production workflow depending on the type of output you need to create. If your images are destined for four-color offset printing, you'll have a very different workflow than if you're simply going to post your images to the Web.

In general, though, your workflow will go something like this:

1. Transfer your images from your media cards to your computer. You can do this directly from your camera, or by using a card reader. If you're out in the field, you'll be better served by using a card reader, so as not to waste battery power.

2. Organize your images into folders. How you want to organize your images is up to you. Some people like to simply throw all of their images from a specific project into one folder or directory. Others like to group them into subfolders by day, or topic. Whatever method you decide to use try to be consistent from one assignment to the next.

3. Identify your select images. You don't want to waste time making corrections to images that you ultimately won't use, either

because you don't like their composition, they're not sharp, or because you simply have a better alternative. So, before you start editing, you'll want to select the "hero" images that you'll pass through the rest of your workflow.

4. Edit your images. At this stage, you can use any editing techniques that you like, and any image editor that provides the tools you need. If you've been following the strategy presented in this book, though, this stage should be fairly short.

5. Output your images. This stage will vary depending on your needs. If you need electronic output for delivery to a service bureau or client, then you'll usually want to deliver flattened images at a particular resolution (and sometimes particular color mode) and in a specific format. Your client or service bureau will provide you with these specifics. If you're printing, then you'll usually print directly from your image editing application. However because printing often requires additional corrections, you might want to create a separate copy of your image specifically for printing.

6. Archive your images. Once the job is finished, you'll want to make sure that your images—original and edited—are safely archived for long-term storage. You can copy your images to additional hard drives, or burn them to CD or DVD. This stage might also include using an image cataloging program such as Microsoft iView Media Pro or Extensis Portfolio to create a browsable catalog of thumbnails of your archived media.

This basic structure is very malleable, and as mentioned earlier, you'll probably need to modify it depending on the needs of a specific job. For example, in some cases you might need to do some additional, intermediate outputs to deliver images to an art director or client for approval. No matter how you alter and adjust this workflow, there are a couple of tips that you should always keep in mind:

■ Never re-compress an image! If you're shooting in JPEG mode, you should never perform an additional JPEG compression until your final output stage, and then only if you need to deliver a JPEG file. Every time you re-save a JPEG file you expose it to more image-degrading JPEG compression. When editing an image, save your edited version in a lossless format such as TIFF or Photoshop (.psd). You can save JPEGs when you're ready to output your edited version for posting to the Web, or email delivery.

- As you develop and refine your workflow, you'll want to be sure that you always use the same naming conventions, organizational schemes and so on. As your image library grows, you'll have an easier time searching and managing it if you've named and organized things consistently.

Fortunately, just as Photoshop makes your traditional darkroom work easier and faster, there are digital tools that also ease your workflow and library management hassles.

Adobe Bridge

If you're using Photoshop CS2, then you also have a copy of Adobe Bridge, a file browser and organizer that can help you make short work of your organizational tasks. Opening and examining lots of documents in Photoshop can be extremely time-consuming—especially if you're working with a camera with a high pixel count. Bridge greatly streamlines your browsing and organizing by letting you view thumbnails of all of the images in a folder (**Figure 9.1**).

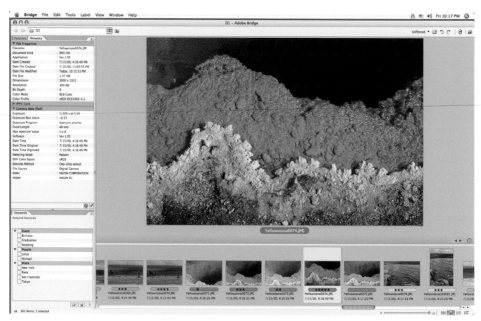

Figure 9.1 Bridge offers a clean and simple means to peruse images. Bridge's three layout options are metadata (left), preview image (top), and filmstrip (bottom).

Using the Folders tab in the upper left corner of the Bridge window, navigate to the folder of images that you want to browse. Bridge will display thumbnails of all of the images in that folder. You can use Bridge to perform your initial organization of your images, and what's more, you can create new folders, move images from folder to folder, and rename images all within Bridge.

You can also use Bridge's Batch Rename command (Tools > Batch Rename) to automatically rename your images. Select the images you want to rename, and then configure the Batch Rename dialog to automatically rename images with sequential numbers, custom text, and more.

These two features take care of the first part of your workflow. Now you're ready to start identifying your select images. In the lower-right corner of the Bridge window you'll find four buttons that let you change the way the currently browsed folder is displayed. Play with these to explore the different options.

You can easily use the arrow keys to navigate through the images in the current folder. When you find one that you want to mark as a select, or "pick" image, you can employ Bridge's ratings feature to distinguish those that are at the top of the list from those that are merely good.

Labeling and rating images

You can rate and color label your images either by using the Label pull-down menu or by hitting a keyboard combination that corresponds to the rating you want: for the Mac, Command (or Control in Windows) plus 1, 2, 3, 4, or 5, indicating how many stars you'd like to assign the photo. For color labels, similarly use, Command (Mac) or Control (Windows) + 6, 7, 8, and 9, or use the pull-down menu to assign different colors. Simply scroll with your arrow keys through your filmstrip of images, or enlarged thumbnails, and Label and Rate your photos. Afterwards, you can filter those images according to how many stars you've given them or by how they've been labeled, by clicking on the Unfiltered pull down menu at the top right of the Bridge window or by using the Sort command under the View menu (**Figure 9.2**).

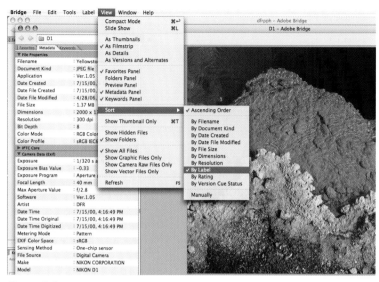

Figure 9.2 Bridge's Sort option allows you to view your images by size, rating, and many other attributes.

A very useful feature of Bridge is the ability to view Thumbnails at large sizes (**Figure 9.3**). Move to the lower right hand corner of the Bridge window and click on the Thumbnails view button. Immediately to the left of this button is a slider that will allow you to enlarge and reduce the size of your thumbnails. When you enlarge your thumbnails to the largest possible setting it allows you to compare your Labeled and Rated images in the same screen. Often during an edit, I first eliminate the images that miss the mark. Then I identify the best with either four or five stars. After filtering out those images with less than four stars

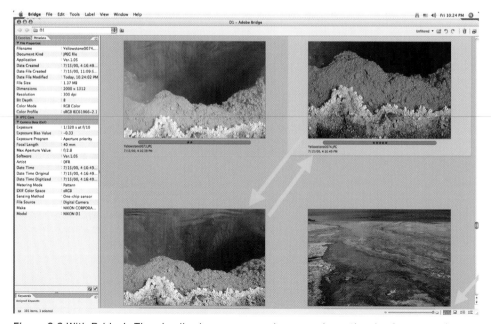

Figure 9.3 With Bridge's Thumbnails view you can reduce or enlarge the size for comparison.

(see the button at the top right hand side of the Bridge window), the large thumbnail view gives me a second look to compare images in a tighter context. In other words, I'm able to put the near misses and mistakes aside and compare only my best images.

The Metadata palette on the left side of the Bridge window lets you edit the metadata for the currently selected image. Click in the field you want to edit, and enter new text. If you tag your images with good metadata, you'll have an easier time with not only your immediate post-production workflow, but with your long-term library management as well. For example, you can use Bridge's metadata features to tag your images with specific locations or subject matter, allowing you to later search for images shot in particular venues, or find all of the images that contain a specific person or subject.

Batch processing files

Batch processing lets you automate certain processing operations to images with similar qualities so you don't have to apply changes to images individually. Using a prototype image, you apply edits to it—for example, rotate the image, sharpen it, change its color mode—and record those transformations as a Photoshop Action that can then be played back to the same effect on another image. To apply the Action to multiple images, you use Photoshop's batch processing features. Bridge lets you batch process images by launching Photoshop and asking you to identify both a Source folder (images you want to batch process) and a Destination folder (location where the batched images will be placed) (**Figure 9.4**). The interface for Batch processing isn't pretty or intuitive, but the time invested in learning how it works is well worth it.

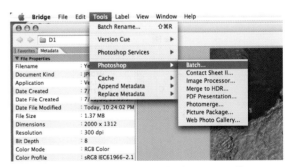

Figure 9.4 Batch processing in Bridge is actually a service of Photoshop. It can save you lots of time by eliminating redundant operations (Actions) on a folder of images.

Let's walk through the Batch process, from creating an Action to applying changes en masse, below:

1. Double click on an image in Bridge to open it in either Camera Raw or Photoshop. (If you initially open a raw image, make the required toning adjustments and Open the image into Photoshop.)

2. Display your Actions window by clicking on Window > Actions or Option-F9 (on a Mac) or Alt-F9 (on Windows).

3. Discover the Default Actions provided in Photoshop, or create your own. For example, sharpening is something we often perform on multiple images headed for the same destination, i.e., perhaps to a particular printer or Web site application.

4. At the upper right hand corner of the Action palette click your mouse on the small arrow to open the flyout menu.

5. Select New Action... from this list of prompts and give it the name (label) you can identify easily in the future. For instance, if you plan to make a sharpening Action for an image being prepared for an Epson Ink Jet printer using matte surface paper, you might name it, "Sharp_Epson 2400_Matte," or whatever label works for you. (You can also create a New Action by clicking on the very small Create new action icon at the lower right hand side of the Action palette.) You can choose where you want to save this Action, either adding it to an existing Action Set or making your own custom Actions set.

6. After testing what settings work and which ones you want to use, create your Action. At the lower center section of the Action palette click on Begin recording (this is a small button that turns red when you click it). From the point it turns red, everything you do in Photoshop will be recorded until you stop—so make sure you take your time and proceed cautiously. Avoid extra steps that you may need to modify or eliminate later.

7. With the red recording indicator on, sharpen your opened image. You will note that each step you take when running this recording process is relayed to the Action palette. You can see each function listed as it's added to the Action. (This is not a time and place to experiment as each act will be recorded within that specific Action.)

8. Once you're satisfied with your sharpening, click on the Stop Recording button at the lower left hand side of the Actions palette. Save your Action and give it a name.

9. Test your Action on another image. With a new image open, go to the Actions palette and click on your saved Action. Click the Play triangle at the bottom on the palette or select Play from the palette's flyout menu. Be sure that your new Action is active, indicated by the checkmark next to its name on the left side of the Actions palette. If it is not checked it will not show as an option when using Photoshop's Batch Tool.

10. To apply your action to multiple images, in Bridge open the group of images that you want the Action to affect.

11. Set up your images for Batch processing by using the pull down menu: Tools > Photoshop > Batch. Once the Batch dialogue box appears you have four choices to make: Play, Source, Destination, and Errors.

12. Play is where you choose which Actions will be applied. First select a Set of Actions. If you want to apply the sharpening Action you just recorded, then select the Set where that Action is saved. Then select the specific action within that Set.

13. Source is where you select which images will be affected by the Action. You can select a folder of images on your hard disk, but in this case since we are accessing Batch through Bridge, the drop-down menu gives you the option to choose Bridge, so that whatever images you have selected in Bridge will have the Action applied to them.

Select the Override Action "Open" Commands if opening the image has been built into the Action as a step. If you like, also click "Include All Subfolders" when there may be images segregated away from others within a folder. I would not choose the "Suppress File Open Options Dialogs" and "Suppress Color Profile Warnings." That's because I know the color profiles of my images and don't want to be interrupted with a "File Open Option."

14. Destination is the folder in which the batched images will be placed after the work is done. I suggest you choose or create a new folder in an effort to organize your images more efficiently. If you have built a Save As step into your Action, go ahead and check Override Action "Save As" Command. Below this option are File Naming fields for names, dates, serial numbers and extensions. If you've named your files in a numeric sequence, you can decide which Serial number to start the batch processing with. And, finally you have the Compatibility option to click on Windows, Mac OS and Unix.

15. Errors is how Photoshop reacts when it finds errors. You have the choice of either stopping for errors, or logging them to a file. Since I usually just get a cup of coffee when batch processing my files, I select Stop For Errors. When an error occurs I must attend to it before proceeding. If, however, you are batch processing overnight or during downtime, you may check Log Errors to File.

16. Finally, click the OK button and let 'er rip! You will see the Photoshop Batch Tool perform Actions on every image in the source folder and place each newly saved image in a destination folder.

Batch processing is just one of the ways Photoshop and Bridge work together to help you manage your images. You can add Camera Raw into the mix, too, as described in Chapter 6, "Processing

Raw Images." So critical is streamlining the raw image work-flow that Adobe has also developed a new product called Adobe Photoshop Lightroom specifically for digital photographers. A similar product from Apple, called Aperture, targets the same type of workflow. Neither Lightroom nor Aperture are substitutes for Photoshop, however, as they do not allow extensive image editing.

Special Image Handling

Sometimes, you'll engage in special shooting practices, such as panoramic photography, that require a separate post-production step. Panoramic photography is the process of shooting a series of overlapping images, and then stitching those images together into one single wide format image or panorama. Photoshop's Photomerge command (File > Automate > Photomerge) does an excellent job of stitching, and you can easily launch images from Bridge directly into the Photomerge command by using Bridge's Tools > Photoshop > Photomerge command.

You'll want to perform this stitching *before* you perform your normal image editing step. Stitching will leave you with another "select" image that you can pass through the rest of your normal workflow.

High Dynamic Range (HDR) Imaging

High-dynamic range (HDR) imaging is a great example of how good photography and good Photoshop work can come together to make wonderful photographs. Instead of relying on one capture to make an image, HDR imaging allows us to combine several captures with different exposure levels into one complete HDR image.

HDR allows you to capture extremely high-contrast motionless scenes, like brilliant landscapes or bright stationary objects against dark backgrounds. There must, however, be no movement within the photographic scene. Most cameras (film or digital) simply can't make sense of extreme contrast like that, and so force you to choose between capturing adequate highlight detail or shadow detail. In HDR imaging, you capture the image in two or more exposures, making sure to get complete shadow and highlight detail, and then combine those captures into one image.

Because HDR images are made up of multiple captures, they contain an enormous amount of information, which translates into great flexibility for subsequent Photoshop work. Some cameras capture over 4,000 levels of gray for each channel—red, green, and blue. HDR images combine all this information into one file. HDR images, in essence, are digital originals with deep amounts of brightness information, sometimes more than you'll even need. Images with a standard dynamic range, such as JPEGs, begin with much less information, which is why making tone adjustments—discarding values in order to create balance—creates a posterizing effect in areas of the image where not enough detail remains. HDR images, on the other hand, work optimally when using raw captures.

The first exposure you make will capture the shadow details of your scene. The second will capture the highlight details. Then, you'll use Photoshop's File > Automate > Merge to HDR command to combine the captures into an image that the camera alone could not have created. Adobe Bridge has an even easier way to do this with two or more HDR images: Tools > Photoshop > Merge to HDR (**Figure 9.5**). The HDR feature in Bridge makes it easy to process a number of images very quickly and is faster than selecting the images using the Merge to HDR commands file selector in Photoshop.

Still, HDR is no panacea for poor photographic skill. HDR photography requires that you use your camera intelligently and effectively. You must know how to interpret and understand your scene's contrast (or lighting ratio) enough to recognize when a scene has a contrast range beyond what the camera can capture in a single exposure. You'll want to maintain detail in your highlights and shadows while still respecting your midtones.

Figure 9.5a The fastest and easiest way to blend your HDR files into one final image is to use Adobe Bridge, which automates a much longer step-by-step procedure you would have to follow in Photoshop.

Figure 9.5b Once two or more images are moved to the Merge to HDR queue, you can begin blending a series of different exposures of the same scene.

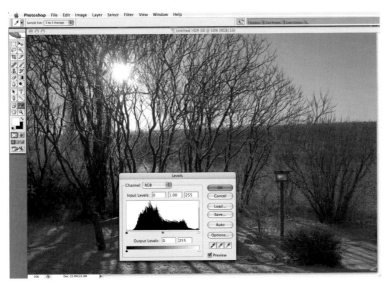

Figure 9.5c Ultimately, you'll have a well-balanced image in terms of tones. HDR blending is an invaluable tool when you are confronted with a photographic scene that has many more tones than can be photographed with one camera exposure.

Preparing for Output

Once you're done editing your selects, or top-ranked images, you're ready to output them in whatever way your workflow demands. In Photoshop, this will probably mean either printing your files for the paper page, or preparing them for electronic delivery. If your ultimate destination is offset printing, then you'll need to talk to your printer or service bureau about specific file specs—color mode, resolution, image format.

If you need to deliver files for Web or email, then you'll want to use Photoshop's Image Size or Fit Image commands to resize the image to something that is a little more network friendly. And, of course, you'll want to save in a compressed format such as JPEG or PNG.

For many photographers, however, the majority of images will end up as a reflective print, transparency, halftone, or color separation for print reproduction. Each of these destinations has unique characteristics in terms of resolution, tonal range, and color, and

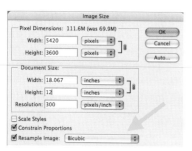

Figure 9.6 Resampling is a powerful function within Adobe RAW and Photoshop. But it must be used with care not to dilute image resolution quality. Most photographers resample using bicubic interpolation.

that arrangement should be on your mind as you prepare for and capture the image. Sometimes, the photographer doesn't know how the image will be used. Or perhaps the client has changed his or her mind along the way. The trick is to make your best educated guess, and select your camera and its settings accordingly.

A photographer should always select his photographic tools based on what he predicts will be the highest resolution any client may require in a photograph. Of course, there's a trade-off: Picture information can be costly in terms of the price of the technology and the increase in the workflow. For instance, an image from a 1-megapixel camera is usually more than sufficient resolution for Web-based images; any more than that isn't just expensive, it's superfluous. This same principle applies to newspaper photojournalism. The vast majority of newspapers today require a 4- to 5-megapixel image. More information, unless you're doing a lot of image cropping, is overkill. A 7- or 8-megapixel image will slow the workflow and impede storage and retrieval. Larger images from higher-resolution cameras take longer to write to a camera's memory system, take longer to make tone adjustments to, and longer to transmit. These can be real obstacles for photojournalists shooting fast-paced sports action events, for example, or working close to a publication's deadline.

On the other hand, the wedding/event photographer, portrait photographer, or advertising photographer often needs all the pixels she can get. Ten- to 54-megapixel cameras are not uncommon, and every one of those pixels goes to good use. A commercial photographer may need to send his images off to make continuous tone (CT) display transparencies with dimensions of four feet or more, and you can't do that without very high resolution.

Enlarging your image in Photoshop

Photoshop's Image Size menu item (Image > Image size; **Figure 9.6**) gives you the option to resample your image to a larger size, and it can be surprising how well this works. To do this, most Photoshop users employ *bicubic interpolation*, a complex algorithm

A ROUGH GUIDE TO RESOLUTION

Each medium has different requirements in terms of resolution. A newspaper image, for example, typically requires far lower resolution than an ink-jet printout, which means that you'll be able to run any given image at a larger size in a newspaper than in an ink-jet print. The lower the resolution requirement, the larger you'll be able to run the image. To determine your maximum print size, just divide the number of pixels along the x- and y-axes of your image by the optimum resolution for your destination medium.

An image that is 2,000 x 3,000 pixels should, for example, print quality images at the following sizes:

For a newspaper (120–160 PPI): 16.5" x 25" down to 12.5" x 18.75"

For a magazine (225–300 PPI): 8.9" x 13.3" down to 6.7" x 10"

For photo paper/film (200 PPI): 10" x 15" (**Figure 9.7**)

For ink-jet paper (360+ PPI): 5.5" x 8.34" or smaller

For photo paper/film (400 PPI): 5" x 7.5"

Figure 9.7 This image is printed at 200 DPI from a Nikon D2Hs camera. The actual print size, of course, is slightly larger than 8" x 12" in size.

that essentially creates new pixels based on neighboring pixels in the image. It uses what's already in the image to interpolate, what would be there in a higher-resolution version.

This technology works amazingly well, but there's a limit to everything. You can only dilute lemonade so much before it tastes more like water than lemonade. Upsize an image too much and you'll lose important scene detail, so be cautious. The amount of resampling you attempt should depend partly on the viewing conditions (i.e., how close your viewer will be to the image), and how discriminating your viewer is likely to be.

When you crop and resize an image, important detail may be lost so always consider your image intentions when shooting the image in the first place (**Figures 9.8** and **9.9**).

Figure 9.8 The detail in this image is strong and clean.

Figure 9.9 A cropped image that's been magnified.

Archiving your Images

When all of your work is through, you'll be ready to back up and archive your images for long-term storage. The easiest and cheapest way to do this is to burn the images to a CD-ROM or DVD ROM using your favorite disk burning software. After burning the disks, you might want to create a catalog of the contents of each disk using a program such as iView MediaPro or Extensis Portfolio. In the future, you can browse these catalogs to find the images that you want, and then copy them back onto your main drive.

For safe keeping, make multiple copies of each disk and remember: no one really knows how long a recordable CD or DVD will last, so you might want to consider migrating your backups to new media every few years, just to be safe.

Summary

Digital photography may start with a shoot, but it doesn't end when the images are edited in Photoshop. There are images to be selected, processed, and archived. Special situations emerge that need special handling. Short timeframes necessitate automatic solutions like batch processing. To work more efficiently and effectively, you need to establish a workflow that suits not only your projects but your approach to them. The more streamlined your workflow is, the more productive you will be.

Index